The Gay Invasion

A Christian Look at the Spreading Homosexual Myth

William D. Rodgers

ACCENT BOOKS
Denver, Colorado

MEMBER OF
EVANGELICAL CHRISTIAN
PULISHERS ASSOCIATION

Second Printing

ACCENT BOOKS
A division of Accent-B/P Publications
12100 W. Sixth Avenue
P.O. Box 15337
Denver, Colorado 80215

Library of Congress Card Number 77-79353

ISBN O-916406-76-8

Acknowledgments

No one writes a book by himself, least of all me. I want to express my deep gratitude to the many who selflessly assisted me in this present undertaking:

To Byron Leech and Amy Ross Young who suggested that I write this book in the first place and then encouraged me while I did so.

To Dr. Robert Mosier, President of Accent Books, who had the courage of his convictions and mine and published this book despite its rather risky nature as a business venture.

To all my friends at Accent Books who supplied to me many of their original research projects in this field and shared with me Christian articles and books pertinent to my subject.

Most of all, to Violet T. Pearson, Accent Executive Editor, who slaved as hard as I to make sense of my sometimes rambling sentence structure. And who took a rather rough manuscript and placed it in a form fit for publication.

To my father and brother, who as my business partners "covered" for me the many hours I was away from the office to pursue my research and writing.

And, finally, to my wife and children who patiently did without a husband and father while I was locked in my den for the many evenings and weekends it took to produce the final draft.

Thank you all.

Contents

All names and places have been changed in the first person accounts in this book to protect the innocent. The incidents, nonetheless, are true.

Prologue

Let me set the record straight at the top.

I am not a psychologist.

I am not a psychiatrist.

I am not gay.

I never was gay.

I am an amateur behaviorist because I need to be in my profession.

I am an evangelical Christian.

I do not hate homosexuals, only the practice of homosexuality.

So what's a nice Christian fellow like me doing, writing a book like this?

I wondered that myself at first. It happened because I opened my big mouth at the wrong time.

I chanced to be in a meeting with some of the folks from Accent Books. They mentioned the fact that they were looking for a few good book-length manuscripts on contemporary themes.

"I know a subject I could write a book on," I blurted.

They looked at me expectantly.

"Homosexuality. I am so sick of having it forced down my throat on television."

"Then why don't you write that book?" they asked.

It turned out they had been searching for an acceptable manuscript on the subject for more than a year. I think they secretly hoped that the Lord would move someone else to publish a book on the subject before they did. It is a topic so fraught with controversy and even danger.

"Can you give us a sample chapter and an outline by early next week?" they asked.

I promised I would think about it, but to myself I said, "Never."

There's a woman in our Sunday School class whose father was a preacher. I've heard her quote him many times. "Never say 'Never' to the Lord," he said. "Because when you say 'Never' the Lord has a way of changing your plans."

He changed mine all right. That week the news was full of stories about homosexuals and their activities. Television outdid itself presenting dramas and melodramas and comedies with homosexual characters in them. I opened a Christian magazine to get away from it and the first thing I turned to was a story about homosexuals in the church.

You don't have to hit me over the head with a club more than ten or twenty times to get my attention. Somebody was trying to tell me something.

I began to think about it. There was more homosexuality portrayed in the media, far more than even I had noticed before. And so much of it was misinformation. People were being confused. They weren't seeing the truth.

And then it struck me. In my abortive career as an actor in my youth, I had known many homosexuals of both sexes. I had seen it firsthand and close-up at least seventeen years before most Christians had been confronted by it so openly. I had had to search the Bible for its teachings on the subject and come to grips with my own attitudes and feelings about it far in advance of when the majority of my fellow believers would be exposed to it in such large doses.

Those had been very trying days in my young life. Now, I began to see why I had faced them and endured. I believe it was a part of God's plan for my life, he was preparing me to share my understanding of homosexuality later on. He was preparing me for this book.

It was a humbling thought. More importantly, whether I wanted to or not, I owed it to Him to make the best of the opportunity He was presenting.

I reached this conclusion on Saturday afternoon. The next Monday I gave the people at Accent Books not one sample chapter but two and an outline of what the book would cover.

On Tuesday, they gave me the go-ahead. The book you now hold in your hands is the result.

It is not intended to be a definitive and final study on homosexuality. I have tried instead to share with you what I know to be the facts about the scope of the Gay Invasion and about the people who are behind it.

Since experts agree that the percentage of crimes committed by homosexuals as a group is about the same as the percentage committed by heterosexuals, I have deliberately stayed away from reporting celebrated cases of homosexual murder and rape. There is enough sensationalism inherent in the subject without letting those dramatic incidents obscure the real issues and the real dangers a growing gay culture poses.

I believe it is time that the spotlight be turned upon the "average" homosexual. It is time we see that they are people like we are, and as people are capable of concern and care, hate and destruction.

For in the Gay Invasion, the homosexuals are the victims as much as the rest of us. Some of these gays helped me write this volume, knowing full well what my position would be. I thank them for their cooperation.

Other information included here comes from my own experience, interviews with experts and from the many books available on the subject. Many of the published sources remain anonymous because I do not want to be guilty of publicizing or inadvertently recommending to Christians any book or magazine which is less than Christian in philosophy.

Finally, remember, this book is not written for the professional counselor or the scholastic intellectual. It is written for Bible-believing Christians and any others who sincerely want to know what they can do in dealing with the homosexual dilemma now thrust upon us. It is a book for laymen by a layman.

I pray it will help.

William D. Rodgers

1
Too Bad About Dick and Jane

"Too bad about Dick."

I nodded not knowing what to say. An uncomfortable feeling had lodged itself in the pit of my stomach, the same feeling that came over me lately whenever Dick's name was mentioned.

"Poor Dick," my friend said. I could not look him in the eye. Instead, I stared out over the Green in front of Old Main. The grass was turning with the expectancy of Spring. The trees stretched forth their budding branches in seeming joy over the warmth of the new season.

I felt no joy. No warmth. Only a cruel coldness.

Dick was a friend of mine and had been since our high school days. We had attended the same church, been active in the same youth group and shared the same interest: theatre.

He was a year ahead of me in school, but we had been close. When he served as president of the church Training Time class, I had been his vice president. He was guileless, and while not handsome, was charming, adored by the girls and he, in turn, genuinely adored them in the Christian tradition that was our heritage.

He displayed a real talent for the technical side of the theatre at the university which we both attended. But Dick wasn't satisfied. He wanted to be an actor, not a technician.

Yet, when I was cast in a major role in the theatre department's first production of my freshman year, Dick displayed no jealousy. On the contrary, as we stood before the bulletin board where the results of the auditions were posted and we found my name and not his, he shrugged and gave me a playful punch on the shoulder with his fist.

"I'll sign up for the lighting crew," he said, "and give you the kind of spotlight a budding star deserves."

Shortly after rehearsals began, Dick was befriended by the professor directing the play. When the actor portraying the lead broke his leg in a freak accident, the director replaced him with Dick.

The role was far beyond Dick's abilities. Some thought it odd that he had been given such a plum, since the department was run on a professional basis. This meant that actors were cast because they fit the role in the same way actors are cast on Broadway or in films.

But there Dick was, bumbling his way through a role he had no business playing. It was wondered at for a time and talked about in backstage whispers until it became apparent that Dick and the professor were far more than just good friends.

Now, you must understand, in the theatre, even university theatre, homosexuality is seldom condemned. Theatre people pride themselves on their liberality; their ability to accept "alternate lifestyles" without enmity.

Certainly there were those, like myself, who were familiar with the Biblical admonitions against sodomy. Yet, we did what so many Christians these days do, we rationalized our position. Dick might be violating the holy laws of God, but we ourselves would never be guilty of such immorality. In our piousness, we even convinced each other there was no point in talking with Dick about his sin. He probably wouldn't listen. He had made his choice. Why cast your pearls before swine?

Once, though, I did speak with Dick about his homosexuality. He fairly bubbled with enthusiasm about what he called, "My new found identity."

When I reminded him of Leviticus 18:22, he smiled. "You stick with the old myths and traditions," he said, "but I've found the truth and the truth has made me free."

And, then, he added, "I owe John (the professor) a lot. If he hadn't showed me the truth about myself, I probably would have gone through life without knowing. Just think! I would have gotten married, had kids, grown old without ever knowing what I was missing."

Shocked? Revolted? Me? You bet, just like you are, I hope.

Still, when you are around something like that for an extended period of time, the devil has a way of pulling the wool over your eyes. You become inured to wickedness. That is what happened to the Jews many times in their history. The Bible tells us about it and warns us about it over and over again.

Dick didn't come back to school after the fall quarter. He was restless, he said. A few thought he looked haunted. Anyway, he said he wanted to give Hollywood a whirl and off he went.

He came back at the beginning of the Spring quarter. There didn't seem to be any particular reason for it. He claimed he was about to get his big "break" in the film capitol, but he had lost weight and didn't look at all well.

The strange thing was, he didn't go to see his old friend, the professor, at all.

One day he was gone again, back to Hollywood they said. Ten days later, they found him in his car beside a lonely stretch of highway between Barstow and Los Angeles. He had shot himself through the head.

Too bad about Dick.

Too bad about Jane.

Jane was the assistant traffic girl at a television station I worked at about three years after I got my degree. She was a chunky little gal in her early twenties. No raving beauty, not even pretty, but she had a nice personality and a nice husband who was the produce manager at a local supermarket.

Jane and Sheila, her boss, spent a lot of time behind closed doors. But no one at the station thought much of it, since that is what traffic managers and their assistants usually do at a broadcast outlet.

There was an elusive rumor or two infrequently making the rounds that Sheila was "that way." I don't think anyone really believed the stories. Sheila was not much liked by her co-workers and the gossip about her merely gave the secretaries and their bosses a little titillating gossip during the coffee breaks. Or, so I thought until the rumors about Sheila were proved true in a most public way.

That's when people remembered the closed-door conferences

between Sheila and Jane. There had never been a hint of scandal about the assistant traffic director. But there was now.

People talked and speculated and talked until they hounded her into resigning her position. She couldn't find another job, either, not in that town. The "truth" about Jane had spread. The fact was, she and her husband had to move completely out of the state before they finally escaped the rumormongers.

My wife and I had known Jane and her husband fairly well. I am convinced she was as normal as any twenty-year-old bride. She was judged guilty only on the strength of a business-hours association and a closed door.

Yes, too bad about Dick and Jane. One was the victim of self-gratification. The other was the victim of someone else's sin. On the surface, tragedy from two different causes; the only common bond is the presence of homosexuality. Or is it really?

The Scripture tells us in I Corinthians 6:9, 10, "Know ye not that the unrighteous shall not inherit the kingdom of God? Be not deceived: neither fornicators, nor idolaters, nor adulterers, nor effeminate, nor abusers of themselves with mankind, nor thieves, nor covetous, nor drunkards, nor revilers [and slanderers], nor extortioners, shall inherit the kingdom of God." ("Slanderers" is a good modern equivalent of "revilers," because, according to the dictionary, the latter means, "to assail with bitter abuse." The term in brackets is added from the Amplified Bible published by Zondervan.)

Homosexuality is clearly linked with slander. And that is as it should be. More than that, all the sins listed in the passage just quoted are part and parcel of a phenomenon that has made its way into world events. It is the Gay Invasion.

Dick and Jane were two of its early victims. Unless we as Christians understand it and deal with it in the strength and truth of our Faith, then we may well become its next victims.

Too bad about us.

2
Sodomites in the Land

One week not long ago, I watched a total of fourteen hours of television. That's not much, really, when you consider that according to the Television Advertisers Bureau, the average viewer in the United States today watches TV more than six hours in every twenty-four hour period.

In the fourteen hours I viewed, I counted a total of fifty-nine references to homosexuality. They ranged from a movie billed as the week's "big event" which dealt with the blackmail of lesbian lovers to burlesque type humor complete with limp-wrists on a late night talk program. In between, there was an episode on a popular detective series about a female homosexual who killed a man because she thought he might steal her partner's love (the same series had aired a script which made a hero of a homosexual male police officer the previous week), an hour devoted to a real-life college professor who became a homosexual only recently (he said it gave his life meaning which his ex-wife and children had not), and several assorted situation comedies and dramatic programs which had homosexual characters and references incidental to the plotlines.

Of course, one purpose of all this abnormal emphasis upon sodomites was and is sensationalism. National networks and local stations alike are in the business of attracting large audiences for their advertisers. The more sensational a program is in the off-beat and the novel, the more viewers it will attract. The more viewers, the more that can be charged for commercial announcement time.

Nor is it confined to just one week's run on the tube. Only recently, a half hour comedy which ran in the eight o'clock time period, a time of the evening when many grade school children are still awake and still viewing TV, took a turn to explicit homosexual jokes ten minutes after it started. I wonder how many parents jumped from their chairs to change channels? I would imagine not many.

Yes, sensationalism is definitely one of the purposes. I used to work in the television industry in the days when the portrayal of a "painted lady" in a Western was about as daring as any network allowed a producer to get. I haven't sat in on any story conferences lately, but I can just imagine the producer of a Western today saying to his writer, "Make the gunfighter a homosexual and it will be worth at least ten more rating points."

But that is not all there is to it. There's a deeper purpose in the glut of abnormality being fed to the American people. That ulterior mission was made quite clear in an article appearing in the Roundup Magazine section of the *Denver Post* one Sunday in the fall of 1976. It said that "some of the major television producers in Hollywood" had agreed to cooperate with the Gay Liberation movement to portray homosexuals "honestly and accurately." The statement is apparently to reinforce Hollywood's promise to *legitimize* homosexuality.

It makes absolutely no difference that the Word of God says, "If a man also lie with mankind, as he lieth with a woman, both of them have committed an abomination: they shall surely be put to death; their blood shall be upon them" (Leviticus 20:13).

God plainly says it's wrong, but man is going to make it right, the thing to do, or at the very least, to tolerate.

And television has been at its task for quite some time. In its infancy, it gave us an "uncle in a dress." We laughed. Much later, it gave us the story of an adolescent boy grappling with his father's homosexuality and accepting it. The critics called that one, "sensitive. A needed portrayal of the homosexual dilemma." More recently, we had the opportunity to watch a two-part, two hour medical drama about a male physician who underwent a "sex-change" operation despite the opposition of his wife, his son and his sister-in-law. It had a happy ending when all realized that the operation was the only thing for the poor creature to do since he was "so uncomfortable as a man." (As incredible as it may seem, many so-called "experts" would deny that such perversion is to be classed "homosexual.")

Not once in the entire two hours were any of the Biblical laws against such aberrant conduct mentioned. And any of the characters who raised a protest against the abomination were represented either as redneck thugs or old-fashioned fuddy-duddies who had lost their lease on compassion.

Christians can, of course, protest all this by writing letters to sponsors, networks, stations and the Federal Communications Commission, the government agency which has jurisdiction over the television airwaves which are supposed to be utilized "in the public good."

If our letter writing seems to have little effect, we must understand that the gay organizations and their sympathizers are flooding the mails with even more letters in favor of the current programming practices.

Thus, we who are appalled by the continual bombardment of unnaturalness can resort to the ultimate protest. We can turn off our television sets. Be warned, though, that ignoring TV probably won't keep us from learning more about homosexuality than we care to know.

For example, pick up your newspaper. The average citizen of the U.S. spends less than thirty minutes a day reading his paper according to the statistics provided by the Radio Advertisers Bureau. However, in that thirty minutes he'll probably run across one or two stories about the very subject he turned off his television set to avoid.

Today's news-in-print might feature a story about a priest heralded for his work with the nation's youth who "has come out of the closet" and declared his homosexuality proudly. The sports page might tell us about a transsexual athlete who is now participating as a woman in events she (he) participated in as a man. And back by the comics, where the kids can be sure to see it, might be the story of a homosexual school teacher who is suing a school system to keep her tenure.

Even the religious section—especially the religious section—is a repository for stories with a gay connotation. In our local paper the Friday religious pages have contained at least one story about homosexuals virtually every week for twelve weeks. While I hadn't kept track before that, I suspect the stories have been appearing consecutively for much longer than the three months I surveyed.

So maybe you'd prefer to read magazines. On second thought, maybe you wouldn't.

One very respected housekeeping magazine has carried such articles as, "My Husband Left Me for a Man" and "My Daughter Is Now My Son." Remember, this is not a cheap confessions publication or a sick-slick from a pornographic distributor, but a widely circulated mainstream women's periodical. And it is just one of many quality publications on the market every month with like material.

The point is, the Gay Invasion is making itself felt in every public medium. Television. Newspapers. Magazines. Books.

The invasion is even evident in children's literature. A book co-authored by a medical psychologist from a most prestigious Eastern university and by a well-known journalist happily reports, "Following the lead of the award-winning book by John Donovan, *I'll Get There, It Better Be Worth the Trip,* several authors have dealt openly with teenage homosexual experiences. In Barbra Wersba's novel, *Run Softly, Go Fast,* ignorance leads adults to panic out of all proportion over a brief homosexual experience of a kind familiar to many adolescents."

Your first temptation, as is mine, is probably to shut your eyes and ears to all this smut and to ignore it completely. Why bother with a world that is fast spinning its way toward destruction?

Jesus, Himself, has charged us with the responsibility. He said, "No man, when he hath lighted a candle, putteth it in a secret place, neither under a bushel, but on a candlestick, that they which come in may see the light" (Luke 11:33).

We have the obligation and the resource to let the light of truth shine on the dark places of wickedness. There is nothing which Satan wants more than for us to hide our candles of righteousness from the sinner, the ignorant and the backslider.

The commission which Christ gave Paul on the road to Damascus should also be our commission, and that is, "To open their eyes, and to turn them from darkness to light, and from the power of Satan unto God, that they may receive forgiveness of sins, and inheritance among them which are sanctified by faith that is in me" (Acts 26:18).

To accomplish our mission, we must therefore come to grips with the facts, so that we may be fully informed of the way in which the great mastermind of the present conspiracy subtly twists truth to his own subversion... "Lest Satan get an advantage of us: for we are not ignorant of his devices" (II Corinthians 2:11).

One of Satan's best gimmicks is the Myth of the Minority. The gays claim that is what they are, a minority. Statistics seem to bear them out. One spokesman for gay rights has lately laid claim to a figure of twenty million homosexuals in the United States. In a country of two hundred million people, that doesn't sound like much. It is only ten percent of the population. On the other hand, that's more people than live in the nation's largest city. The number of homosexuals in America today would fill four hundred football stadiums each holding fifty thousand people!

Suddenly, the "minority" doesn't seem so small. The homosexual movement is a large one. And, it is exerting pressure to grow even larger this very moment. It may well succeed, for a little homosexuality can go a long way.

As a researcher sympathetic to the movement writes, "In general, it can be said that where homosexuality is lauded, or even merely approved, it tends to be prevalent....."

A little later on, the same researcher says, "...there are a number of these societies in which homosexuality is known to be relatively rare, sometimes very rare, and yet if an adroit homosexual...should come along and introduce 'the practice' to a few men in their teens and twenties, it may catch on like wildfire—or, as is most often the case, it may simply be quietly and quickly accepted by seemingly any man."

And there are sodomites in the land.

3
As in the Days of Lot

I like the word "sodomy." It is one of the few words in the English language which not only names something, but which describes the ramifications of the act it so aptly defines.

To use it is to tell the story of Lot and his guests as found in Genesis 18 and 19. With just six letters, it calls to mind the sex-charged mood of the men in the mob who stood before Lot's door that night, one of the darkest in human history. Their unnatural intent—to homosexually assault the visitors under Lot's protection—was so strong, that even when Lot offered them his own virginal daughters, the men of Sodom reacted with violent perversion, their abnormal lust stubbornly intensified.

And when you call that lust "sodomy," you also call to mind the fiery destruction of divine retribution which came upon that self-same mob and all its associates as a direct result of their actions. Use the word, and you can almost smell the wretching smoke and taste the bitter brimstone.

Yes, sodomy is an excellent word. But to many in the vanguard of the Sexual Revolution it seems too harsh, too distasteful, too cruel to those "unfortunates" it so appropriately convicts. Thus, it has become an anachronistic term unseemly in the vocabularies of our "enlightened" generations. We have purged it from everyday use and relegated it to obscure legal service.

Several states and the District of Columbia still carry statutes against sodomy on their books, but even here it is fast fading from fashion as liberal legislatures find more acceptable nomenclature to sooth the ears of their constituents.

As proof of just how out-of-date sodomy has become, many of the new and most complete paperback dictionaries do not even carry an entry for it. I have several of these dictionaries in my library, but I had to resort to my old reliable Webster's Unabridged before I could find its definition.

Since your dictionary may be like most of mine, let me share the full meaning with you. The Unabridged says, "sod'om-y, n. any sexual intercourse regarded as abnormal, as between persons of the same sex, especially males, or between a person and an animal."

That really says it, doesn't it? It says it too well, so we have resorted to the substitution of more gentle euphemisms which serve to cloud the issue, rather than to make it crystal clear.

There are more than a few homosexuals who, aside from their perversion, have many likable qualities just as there are many likable alcoholics and liars and even murderers. After all, they are people. Many work in respectable professions and publicly conduct themselves with aplomb. Many have made valid contributions to society in their chosen fields of endeavor. Many number heterosexuals among their closest friends, heterosexuals who either do not suspect the homosexual side or choose to ignore it.

Oh, how hard and often painful it is to even think of these affable individuals as "sodomites." Yet, label them that we must for God has said, "There is a way that seemeth right unto a man, but the end thereof are the ways of death" (Proverbs 16:25).

So, while it may be hard and seem cruel, while the right way may seem to be tolerance of another's private preference, we cannot allow ourselves to be hoodwinked by our own misplaced compassion.

Even as I write these words, I feel that I am betraying kindnesses shown me during my theatre days by gay individuals who gave me help and encouragement, not out of any perverted interests, but out of genuine concern for a fellow being's welfare.

The truth of the matter is, that in all the years I pursued the acting profession I never once was personally touched by an untoward advance on the part of any homosexual individual.

I used to wonder at it, why I was spared when other heterosexual thespians reported such advances commonplace? I believe the answer is in Christ's prayer, "I pray not that thou shouldest take them out of the world, but that thou shouldest keep them from evil" (John 17:15).

We find the same thought expressed again in II Thessalonians 3:3, which reads, "But the Lord is faithful, who shall stablish you, and keep you from evil."

He kept me from evil because He had other plans for my life. How grateful I am to Him. How humble I feel before His majesty.

And while I was untouched by it, I was also profoundly touched. You do not, cannot live with something like that day after day, week after week, year after year without feeling its effect.

It was the thing which eventually drove me from the theatre. I was forever saddened and revulsed by the whisperings and titterings that went on in the dressing room before and after every performance. I came to despise the director who brought his boyfriend to every rehearsal. I was like the man who lived near the sewage treatment plant. He was sickened by the stench which continually filled his nostrils and clung to his clothing, but he so loved his home he could not bear to think of moving.

Life upon the stage need not be wicked. There are many fine Christian individuals at all levels of the entertainment industry, but they are in a dwindling minority.

Neither is the theatre any more or less evil than other institutions in the world today. I hold to the conviction that the stage and the people who practice its profession merely anticipate the rest of society. The evil found within it is a mirror of what will be found in the rest of the world in the near future unless and until the tide of the Gay Invasion is turned.

Remember, it was not many decades ago that mothers took steps to protect their daughters when a touring company of show business people came to town because of the promiscuous reputation accorded to actors with members of the opposite sex.

How times change. And how difficult it is to escape that change.

An actor to whom I'm quite close, quit the theatre because of the burgeoning perversity. He applied for a job with a large corporation.

He was interviewed by a portly gentleman with thinning

22

hair who constantly smoked a large cigar. The man was known for his leadership in the community and served on the advisory board of one of America's largest Protestant denominations. He would be the ex-actor's superior, if the latter was hired.

The interview took place in the corporate board room on a Saturday morning. The building was virtually deserted. There were no phones. No interruptions. And so the interview proceeded at a more leisurely pace than would have otherwise been the case.

They talked about the actor's qualifications, of course, and about the specifics of the job for which he was under consideration. They talked about benefits and salary and business philosophy, but they also discussed a wide variety of other things which were non-job related. The topics covered sports, theatre and families.

The actor began to feel he was coming to know this businessman who had won almost every honor and accolade his industry awarded. The businessman was a veteran. He was married. His wife was active in all the best church and social causes. They had six children, two of which were adopted. The businessman took out his wallet and proudly displayed pictures of his sons and daughters, boasting of their accomplishments in school.

"He was a nice guy," the actor recalled later, "a refreshing change from some of the people I had been around."

Finally, the businessman snuffed out the stub of his cigar in an ashtray, took another cigar from his pocket and carefully regarded the actor as he unwrapped the cellophane from the fresh stogie.

"You seem to have a very promising career on the stage," he observed at length. "Tell me, why would you want to give all that up for a position with this company? We have no glamour and very little applause."

By now, the actor felt he could speak bluntly. "The truth is, I love acting," he said, "but I can't stand being around the homosexuals any longer."

The businessman gave an understanding nod and then, with a quick smile said, "You're hired!"

The actor had not been in his new job long before he began to hear rumors that his new boss was gay. He placed absolutely no credence in the tales. Had not the businessman shared his prejudice openly, even approved of it? And demonstrated that approval by hiring him immediately upon the direct expression of the reason as to why the actor had severed his ties to the theatre?

No, the actor could not believe those stories. He marked them down to professional jealousy, and gave them not a second thought. When approached with the gossip directly, he would always quickly counter with the story of the interview. There was the evidence for the vindication of his employer.

Possessing as large a talent for business as he did for drama, the actor was soon on his way up the corporate ladder. He was eventually made the Public Relations Director for the company's largest branch office in another city.

A year later, his former boss, by now Executive Vice President and General Manager of the entire organization, passed through town on his way back from inspecting the corporation's foreign operations. A gala dinner was given to introduce the man to the influential members of the community.

Afterwards, some of the city's most important people took the VIP on a tour of several of the better nightclubs. The former actor was middle-management, so he was not considered important enough to invite along.

At 2 a.m., the phone on the nightstand summoned him from a deep sleep. It was the branch manager who demanded angrily, "Why didn't you tell me your former boss was gay?"

"But he isn't," the actor protested. "I have proof."

"Yeah? Well I have witnesses that he is," the branch manager boiled. "He just made an advance toward the Vice-Mayor in front of the Managing Editor of the morning paper!"

To this day, the actor shakes his head with woeful disbelief. "You just don't know sometimes," he says. "You just don't know."

But...."Shall not God search this out? for he knoweth the secrets of the heart" (Psalms 44:21).

The Lord is not fooled by the outer appearances of the

actor's employer—the service to his church, his country and his industry, the pride in his children, the success, the facade of upper-middle-class respectability. The Lord sees the sin.

We are left with scandalized surprise and puzzlement over how a man with a wife and children can possibly be gay. The answer is, there is a variety of homosexual types.

The businessman above is either a *bisexual* or he is what is commonly referred to as a *"closet gay."*

A bisexual is an individual who is sexually attracted to members of both sexes. They are quite often married people who are able to have a full relationship with their marriage partner while being involved in same-sex relationships on the side—a kind of perverted adultery. Or, the bisexual may alternate between periods of exclusive heterosexual and exclusive homosexual activities as circumstance and inner-mood dictate. The men of Sodom probably practiced bisexuality—they could function in the traditional male-female pattern. That's why Lot attempted to buy them off by offering his daughters, but they much favored desecrated passion.

It is interesting to note that the sins of Sodom spring anew from time to time in the Near East. The mighty prophets of the Old Testament witnessed revivals of debauchery. Isaiah, for example, addressed the important men of his day as "Ye rulers of Sodom" (Isaiah 1:10). And today, there are certain Moslem sects who place a heavy emphasis upon homosexuality. Strangely, these same sects have some of the highest birthrates in the world!

The "closet gays," hide their homosexuality as much as possible from society. They fear society's censure. They attempt to conceal what they are from public view by adopting heterosexual guises. They may marry, even carry on a semblence of a heterosexual relationship, but their real desire is altogether same-sex directed.

Then, there are the *overt gays,* the effeminate men and masculine women. These are the people we probably think of first when the subject of homosexuality is raised.

The men tend to wear silky and colorful clothing. They adorn themselves with jewelry: chokers, necklaces, chains and rings of all types. The more gaudy, the more ostentatious, the better. The practice of wearing a single earring used to be common among them, but has lately fallen out of favor. Their hair is meticulously groomed. Their movements are womanly to the point of exaggeration. Among themselves, they call each other "she" and adopt women's names. But they wish to be perceived as men, albeit womanish men, but men.

The women in this category choose rough, heavy, masculine clothing. They use no feminine adornment, no cosmetics. They frequently wear leather jackets and men's pants and boots. Their hair is short-cropped in a manly fashion. Sometimes, their demeanor is belligerent in imitation of a man's aggressiveness. They are insanely jealous of their lovers. If they wear dresses, their movements are still manish, ungraceful. Yet, they pride themselves on being women.

However, too much emphasis on stereotypes can be deceiving. Overt homosexual men can be found, and commonly, who accent their masculinity rather than camouflage it. Their clothing choice may center around leather and other coarse fabrics. They worship their own slim and muscular bodies. They wear their hair short and are well-groomed. Women think of them as "gorgeous," vital specimens of healthy manhood, but they are men's men and that is precisely the trouble.

Lesbians who play up their supra-femininity are not thought to be as commonplace, but there are more than a few. In both men and women, the importance of these homosexuals who stress their God-given gender is to give the movement a certain look of respectability to the outsider, a "normalness" which serves to make it all more acceptable to ordinary mankind.

Also a part of the homosexual sub-culture are the *transvestites*. These are the men who dress like women and the women who dress like men. Behaviorists differentiate between the effeminate homosexual men and masculine homosexual women and the transvestite because in the former groups there is never an attempt to hide the correct gender identity. The transvestite, on the other hand, makes every effort to masquerade as a member of the opposite sex.

There are two basic types of transvestites: the gay who

attires himself as a woman, or the woman who dresses as a man to be attractive as a sexual object to members of their own sex; and the disturbed individual who satisfies some dark need by cross-dressing. In the last instance, the transvestite may participate in a heterosexual relationship while appearing in his or her unnatural wardrobe. The fact is, they may claim to be normal heterosexuals with their only concession to perversion the desire to clothe themselves as the object of their accord.

No matter. The Bible deals with all forms of transvestism with this simple statement: "The woman shall not wear that which pertaineth unto a man, neither shall a man put on a woman's garment: for all that do so are abomination unto the Lord thy God" (Deuteronomy 22:5).

Now, Biblical expositors occasionally explain that "abomination" means "hateful action toward God." Actually, the connotation goes much further. To the sense of "hateful" we must add the thought of "extreme aversion." God has an aversion to cross-dressing. He finds it detestable in extremity.

Matthew Henry amplifies the law this way in his famous *Commentary on the Whole Bible:* "The distinction of sexes by the apparel is to be kept up, for preservation of our own and our neighbour's chastity... It forbids the confounding of the dispositions and affairs of the sexes...Probably this confounding of garments had been used to gain the opportunity of committing uncleanness, and is therefore forbidden."

The conventions of style and taste play important roles in determining our notions of male and female garb. And these are constantly changing. In the late seventeenth and early eighteenth centuries, at the time Matthew Henry penned the words quoted above, men wore silk breeches and curled wigs with bows and lace.

George Washington wore a powdered wig and outfits which would now be considered "sissy" at best, but in his day, he was the model of American manhood.

Admittedly, the unflagging trend towards the "unisex" look has blurred the lines between male and female fashion. And it shows no sign of abatement. A marketing expert recently told me that the fastest growing category in the field of cosmetics is those for men. He predicted eyeshadow and lip gloss would be as common on men as they are on women!

The extreme form of transvestism is *transsexualism*. A transsexual is a member of one sex who feels they really belong to the other sex. They often describe it as "being a man trapped in a woman's body" or vice versa. Thus, they are willing to endure painful surgery and massive shots of the proper hormone to change their sex. And it is all merely an allusion.

A Christian physician offered an explanation which recalls certain things you probably learned in your high school biology class.

Each embryo, he said, begins as a single fertile cell. The cell contains 23 chromosomes from the mother and 23 from the father. These are God's building supplies which He uses to make an individual that is unique from all others.

The chromosomes are matched to determine the color of hair and eyes, God-given talents and genetic sex. The mother always contributes an "X" sex chromosome. The father can contribute either an "X" or a "Y" sex chromosome. An X and Y paired make a male; two X's make a girl.

Surgery can change the body's appearance, particularly when supplemented with massive doses of sex hormones. But neither surgery nor hormone injections can change genetic sex. A man may look like a woman, but he is still a man. He cannot fulfill the woman's role as a bearer of children, anymore than the genetic woman who has been made to appear a man can father them.

The Bible says, "...male and female created he them" (Genesis 1:27). Man may try to alter God's basic scheme, but he cannot change the fundamental nature of it.

For a long while, transsexual surgery was not performed in the United States. But the barriers of religious, moral and ethical objections have been broken down. Sex change operations are now carried out at such locations as the medical center at Johns Hopkins University and in city and state hospitals supported by your tax dollars and mine. And it is my understanding that it is even covered by some health and medical insurance companies in their policies.

Our legal system, too, has come to recognize the transsexual phenomenon. It is possible for these creatures to have the designation of sex changed on their own birth certificates, to marry as the sex of their choice and to adopt children.

So, there you are. The four basic categories of the gay "race." We are led to believe there is little empathy and discussion exchanged between them. And, the homosexual male may, indeed, find little in common with the homosexual females besides their gayness. Both male and female homosexuals who worship the body of their own sex, find it almost impossible to understand the transsexual who mutilates the very body the homosexual of his gender worships.

But be not fooled by such claims. For if the homosexuals of various types agree in nothing else, they agree in one purpose: they want society's approval of their abnormal lusts. They expect to win that approval by getting the world to forget the laws of the God who created it.

Homosexuality. Bisexuality. Transvestism. Transsexualism.

Could the days of Lot have been any worse?

4
Turning of Things Upside Down

Whenever the subject of homosexuality comes up in secular conversation, it isn't too long before someone is calling upon the theories of Freud, Ellis and Kinsey. Look out, for these three are the unholy trinity of the Gay Invasion. All are long dead. But their theories are alive and kicking. And they have collectively contributed more to modern confusion about the acceptability or unacceptability of homosexuality than all other postulations combined.

Thus, if we are going to understand the complete scope of the Gay Invasion now upon us, we must understand just what it was that these grandfathers of intellectual gobbledygook said about the subject.

In 1881, the University of Vienna's medical school graduated a little fellow with a comic-opera name, Sigmund Freud. Despite a Jewish heritage, Freud was an atheist. As he looked at the world around him, he saw inexplicable incongruity in his fellow humans and felt inconsistent feelings within himself.

Why should people feel guilty over the things they did? He must have wondered. Why should they agonize over them? Why should they make themselves sick with self-blame? Why should man be ashamed?

Freud had his share of what we now call "hang-ups." He could not bear to blame himself, or so it seems, and so, he began to rationalize his mental ills and the ills of others.

That rationalization led to the theory of psycho-analysis. He said it was "a method of treatment for those suffering from nervous disorders."

The chief motivation of the human race, Freud came to believe, was sexual gratification, albeit, an unconscious compulsion. Society and the prohibitions it raised, suppressed fulfillment of man's erotic desires and, therefore, man was made unhappy. When the war between unconscious drives and the repression of society was left unresolved, the result was the anarchy of personality, neurosis.

Man must be permitted to satisfy his hidden gratifications, Freud expounded. Since there was no God, since there was no real reason to mankind's existence, anything and everything should be permitted for the sake of the individual's mental health.

When it came to homosexuality, Freud began with the premise that all children were "incestuous." That in males particularly, the boychild might become so strongly attached to his mother, he identified with her rather than his father. Freud named this situation "the Oedipus Complex" after the tragic hero of the Greek play, *Oedipus Rex.* In the drama, Oedipus killed his father so he might marry his mother.

The Oedipus Complex, Freud thought, led to a transitory period of homosexuality in all children. The boy sought other males as substitutes for himself; males that he could love as he was loved by his mother. A child who had a retarded case of psyche development at this stage, became an adult homosexual.

In other words, Freud said homosexuality was a mental disorder acquired from a domineering mother. He arrived at this conclusion by interviewing his patients and analyzing their dreams.

His theory was quite a revelation to a Victorian society who, for the most part, thought of homosexuality as a debauchery.

Freud made homosexuality something you blamed on your mother.

That conclusion got Freud into intellectual trouble with one of his students, a certain English gentleman of letters, Havelock Ellis. Ellis himself was possessed not only of a "contrary sexual feeling" (a Victorian term for one who was gay), but he was an enthusiast for motherhood, among other things. Those other things included a fervor for sexual experimentation and an abiding desire to understand sexual deviance. Maybe that's why he married a female homosexual.

At any rate, Ellis gave Freud's postulation a second thought and decided he was not at all satisfied with the theory which was fast being embraced with enthusiasm by the world's intelligentsia. If homosexuality was a mother's responsibility, as the good doctor from Austria said, it did great damage to the institution of motherhood; too much damage, it seems, to please Ellis. Freudian theory also gave credence to the notion that homosexuality was an acquired condition and that implied some culpability on the part of the homosexual. It wouldn't do. It just wouldn't do at all.

Ellis therefore set about to contrive an elaborate defense of sexual aberrations, which some believe was a justification of his own perversion. When he apologized for all, he apologized for himself.

At any rate, we do know his lifelong objective was to broaden the scope of sexual tolerance. He began with his book, *Sexual Inversion.* He later condensed the volume into a sex manual for students which he prepared in the early 1930s.

In this latter volume he wrote, "It [homosexuality] is a highly abnormal aberration, and yet it seems to supply a greater satisfaction than any other aberration can furnish." He said it contained all the elements which appeal to human affection. And that it was an important part of the human condition for three reasons: the large and diverse place it occupied in the various historical eras of mankind, the big part it held in contemporary society, and the great number of notable people who subscribed to its practices.

Among the famous homosexuals he pointed to were Desiderius Erasmus, the Dutch humanist, scholar and author of the sixteenth century; Michelangelo, the man whose great works of art include the famous statue of Moses; Christopher Marlowe, the English dramatist and poet; Francis Bacon, the English essayist and statesman; Lord Byron, another English poet of great renown; Oscar Wilde, the British playwright of the last century; and American poet, Walt Whitman. There is no doubt all of these men made brilliant contributions to the world's statesmanship, poetry, art and literature. But Ellis seemed to say, along with all the other proponents of historical homosexuality, these personages accomplished their great works because of their gayness, rather than in spite of it. If that argument is valid, does not it negate the very assertion put forth by the present Gay Liberationists that we should accept them for the attributes and talents they have outside of their homosexuality?

Ellis was an avid reader and supporter of Charles Darwin and his theory of evolution. So the reader of Ellis' tome on sexual inversion soon found the author refuting his own statement that homosexuality was merely a harmless departure from the norm. He was really asserting that it was a simple exaggeration of the statistical average of sexual behavior.

Put another way, he was saying homosexuality was not debauchery and not a mental disorder; sexual inverts were born that way, not made that way. To support his contention, he used the observations of zoologists who claimed to have witnessed homosexual behavior among the primates—chimpanzees, gorillas and baboons. If it is "natural" in the animal kingdom, he lectured, it is consequently "natural" in man.

Ellis said if animals do it, man can do it. Even he realized that zoological evidence in and of itself was not enough. So, he also supported his presumption with case histories of thirty-three male homosexuals and six lesbians, all carefully selected from the best circles of American and British scientific and intellectual communities. Ellis, you see, continually strived to make homosexuality palatable to social taste.

He had to admit that his sample was far too small to serve as a universal statistical base, but then he went boldly ahead and applied his findings to all of humanity.

The case histories he selected are interesting for still another reason. He had a decided tendency to make heroes of the sexual inverts. A small minority of the biographies he reported dealt with individuals who rejected their sexual inversion. These people as portrayed by Ellis' editing, displayed heroic courage in battling their unnatural lusts. They often managed admirable self-control, but always at the cost of exceeding unhappiness. Conversely, those who accepted their sexual inversion seemed ever the more heroic and much more contented with their lot.

Ellis was biased, but he was a good writer and to a medical and scientific community already embracing Darwin and Freud, his conclusions appeared sound. The idea of congenital homosexuality made sense.

If Freud had made homosexuality your mother's fault, by implication Ellis made it God's.

And, although the theories of Freud and Ellis made dents in academic and professional spheres, they had little effect with the masses. That influence was to be brought to bear in a most spectacular manner from a most unexpected source: a taxonomist from the University of Indiana. (In zoology, a taxonomist is one who classifies animals and insects.)

His name was Alfred Kinsey. His major claim to fame was that he had spent twenty years studying, classifying and writing about gallflies. He published two massive volumes on his findings and then turned from bugs to human sexuality.

In 1948 he published his first bestseller in his new field of endeavor, *Sexual Behavior in the Human Male.* It was based upon interviews with 5,300 American men who apparently had told Kinsey and his associates "all" about their most intimate lives in single interviews lasting no more than two hours.

Five years later in 1953, Kinsey authored another book with a similar title based upon the same kind of interviews with 5,940 females. Together, these volumes have become known as "the Kinsey Reports." Outside of the Bible, no two books have so revolutionized the public's attitude toward sexual practices.

In the 1950 census, the population of the U.S. was counted to be almost one hundred and fifty-one million people. Kinsey's sample was 0.00744 of one percent of that population (about seven hundred-thousandths of the population, or one person out of every 14,286!). Yet in the minds of many it was a valid reflection of the sexual life of all citizens of the United States.

The studies of human behavior based upon random sampling have always had one problem—their very randomness. Statisticians build elaborate mathematical models to assure chance selection of participants. What that means is, a television survey company may be told by its computer after evaluation of the raw data, that if the research is to be mathematically valid, it must have interviews from every fifth house on your block. It makes no difference as to the personality of the people that live in those houses. They may be devout Christians or avid atheists. They may have prejudices which bear no relation to the prejudices common in your locale. They may not even watch as much television as everyone else on the block does. It makes no matter. They will represent you and your neighbors by the numbers in the final study.

Of course, research companies recognize the margin of error inherent in their methodology, so they build in plus and minus tolerances. But the people who interpret the data, like TV station managers and network executives, are sometimes not as aware of this as the company which has assembled the actual survey. They don't consider the pluses and minuses. They take the survey as fact.

To demonstrate the pitfalls in the extension of random sampling to measure behavior, let me cite an example of which I have first-hand knowledge.

While I tried to forge a career as an actor, I worked in advertising and later in broadcasting. When I finally decided to put the footlights forever behind me, I went into the advertising agency business. Along with my father and brother, I now own a reasonably successful small agency in Denver.

Recently, we conducted a survey of television viewing habits in our city at the same time another research firm was conducting a study of those same habits. Both firms contacted different random samples of over five hundred homes. We both used the same plus and minus tolerance factors. But their findings and ours were completely opposite. Out of more than five hundred interviews the difference came down to the answers given by twenty-five people. Twenty-five of their respondents gave different responses than twenty-five of ours. Yet when the sample findings were multiplied out to represent the one and a half million people who reside in Denver, the disparities seemed enormous. And, if they had randomly selected twenty-five people other than the ones they did, or if we had, the results would probably have been different still.

Random sampling is far from an exact science. About the only conclusion you can accurately draw from research results is, "Maybe it is that way and maybe it isn't." All other inferences are educated guesswork at best.

I have, of course, simplified this explanation of research methodology a great deal to make it more understandable. But you get the idea.

And random sampling has come a long way since the forties and fifties when Kinsey published his findings. His technique was far superior to those employed by Freud and Ellis, but it left a lot to be desired even for the state of the art in his day.

The first failing in Kinsey's research was that it was based on the recall method. In the two-hour interview, his subjects were asked to remember and report all sexual incidents in their lives. This technique is open to criticism on two counts: people may deliberately lie or their memories may be inaccurate.

Secondly, Kinsey's sample was far from universal. It was made up of volunteers—only those people who wanted to talk about their sexual pasts. It also contained too many homosexuals, too many prison inmates and too many Midwesterners.

It has been suggested that Kinsey had a lot of axes to grind, too. He thought the Judeo-Christian morality was meaningless. In fact, he was at war with our Judeo-Christian heritage. He hated the church and anything associated with it. He thought it perpetuated injustice in our time.

And, too, there seems to be an undeniable prejudice against women in Kinsey's writing and theorizing. He vilified women of all ages as social repressors because of their alignment with educational and religious institutions.

But by far, Kinsey's most outrageous bias was to deny the absolute existence of homosexuality as a category of human behavior. He said that the ability to respond to homosexual stimuli existed in every member of the human species. It was his contention that we are all bisexual and therefore the preference for the same sex is as normal as the preference for the opposite sex.

Well, he said it, so he had to make it true. He set about undermining the notion of sexual identity. *His* figures showed, he said (and I have no doubt they did), thirty-seven percent of the male population had committed at least one homosexual act and fifty percent had responded at some time in their lives to a homosexual motivation.

However, since there was no homosexuality as such in Kinsey's view, he found it hard to write about the subject. So he suggested that the standard terms of heterosexual, homosexual and bisexual be replaced with classification numbers. He came up with a seven-way scale by which to classify a person. It went from 0 to 6. A person who ranked as an 0 was exclusively heterosexual; a 6 was someone who was exclusively homosexual. The mid-point on the scale was 3 denoting a person equally homosexual and heterosexual.

The idea was, you wouldn't say someone was "gay," you'd say he was a "6." The scale never caught on. Too bad that some of the rest of Kinsey's concepts did.

Kinsey's emphasis was not homosexuality alone. He seemed to be anxious to pull down all the social prohibitions against sexual activity of any kind. His statistics were the tools he calculated to use to tumble the walls.

He advanced the claim, for example, that eighty-five percent of married men had had pre-marital sex and fifty percent were unfaithful to their wives. He was very fond of fifty percents.

And he was fond of casting the upper and middle classes in the roles of sexual fascists who enslaved the lower classes with dictated decency. Left to their own inventions, Kinsey opined, the oppressed would create a kind of Peoples Republic of the Boudoir.

No, his emphasis was not homosexuality alone. But it was the area where his ideology had the most original impact. Some say he is credited with creating a more tolerant attitude toward homosexuality; that he was one of the closest friends homosexuals ever had; that his fuzzy thinking on bisexuality still has its "political uses" in advancing the gay cause.

So there you are. Freud made it psychology. Ellis made it congenital. Kinsey made it statistically popular. All of the sexologists of modern times have borrowed from one or all of these perverse pioneers. For instance, Ellis' original idea that gays are born, not made, is still very much in evidence in "scientific thought." Researchers have been searching for the chromosomal proof for almost half a century. They have yet to find it.

But the homosexual apologists keep right on looking and keep on talking as if the proof already exists.

Debates about the cause of homosexuality continue, even among those sympathetic to the gays. About the only thing they can agree on among themselves is that the Bible is wrong on the subject, while man in his "superior wisdom" and secular mercy just has to be right.

Guilt and inhibitions are destructive forces they say. The Bible says men are guilty, therefore the keystone of Judeo-Christian tradition should be rewritten. The church says men sin, therefore the church should be done away with as an archaic institution.

They have turned good to evil and evil to good. But what do we expect? It's the carefully fostered style in our culture.

Yet in the early spring of 1977, a newspaper carried the remarks of Christopher Lasch, professor of history at the University of Rochester and author of several books on social history. Lasch lamented that parents were not imposing their own standards of right and wrong upon their offspring. He said that the doctrines of progressive education and modern psychiatry had confused parents who now made an effort to "understand the needs" of their children instead of guiding them in the matters of right and wrong.

He said this caused the youth to grow up without forming lasting identifications with their fathers and mothers. The fact seemed to sadden Lasch, since he felt that it was "precisely these identifications" which establish the basis of conscience, the thing which leads to an understanding of cultural prohibitions and makes it a moral duty to support and practice them. Thus, he said, the children grow to be adults who care not about the approval of others, but concentrate on their own pleasures. The result leaves children "with a feeling not of liberation but of inner emptiness."

There was a parallel to our times in the tiny country of Judah twenty-five hundred years ago. Homosexuality was rampant. Male prostitutes were everywhere. (They called them "dogs" in those days.) Men expounded on the emptiness of the human condition. They sought answers from astrology. They imported scientists from Babylon. Politicians gave speeches saying their party had "the answer." And while the country seemed to be falling apart internally, the mighty Assyrian army was gradually coming towards it from the North. Northern Israel, Judah's sister nation, fell. Then Samaria and the rest of Israel with her. Judah was frightened. She was next.

And then the prophet Isaiah stood in the streets before the Temple and preached a sermon that told the people exactly what was wrong with their country.

"...The priest and the prophet have erred through strong drink, they are swallowed up of wine, they are out of the way through strong drink; they err in vision, they stumble in judgment... But the word of the Lord was unto them precept upon precept, precept upon precept; line upon line, line upon line; here a little, and there a little; that they might go, and fall backward, and be broken, and snared, and taken" (Isaiah 28:7, 13).

H.A. Ironside, the Bible teacher and preacher who was the pastor of the famous Moody Memorial Church in Chicago for many years, gave great illumination to this passage in his *Expository Notes on the Prophet Isaiah*. He said, "Drunkenness, in Scripture, is often used to illustrate or represent the effects of spiritual intoxication brought about by refusing obedience to the Word of the Lord and giving heed to false teaching."

Like the people of Isaiah's day, we are drunk on false knowledge. We have paid our homage not to God, but to men.

How do we know Freud and Ellis and Kinsey and those who have come after them are false teachers?

As I prepared to write this chapter, someone said to me, "You must be quite knowledgeable to take on such intellectual giants. I don't think I'd be brave enough for that."

There is no courage involved. I'm no smarter than the next

guy. But I do know one thing. Anyone who arrives at the conclusion that something which God says is wrong is right, has to have a theory that is full of holes.

Peter wrote, "... There shall be false teachers among you, who privily shall bring in damnable heresies, even denying the Lord that bought them, and bring upon themselves swift destruction. And many shall follow their pernicious ways; by reason of whom the way of truth shall be evil spoken of" (II Peter 2:1,2).

Paul at once both condemned the works of them that would teach other than the truth and named the author of their suppositions when he called their teachings "doctrines of devils."

We are drunk with knowledge and, as drunkards, we are confused. Parents are confused. Their children are confused.

The day after the newspaper quoted Professor Lasch, Ann Landers published a letter in her syndicated column from a nineteen-year-old college boy.

The boy said that when he entered college the year before, he was unaware of any bisexual relationships among his peers. But as he wrote the letter, bisexuality had grown to become widely accepted and widely practiced by his acquaintances who represented campus leaders from the areas of student government and athletics.

He went on to relate that values taught him in his childhood indicated the practice of bisexuality to be wrong. He claimed he had no real desire to try it, but since his classmates claimed that it "gave them the best of both worlds," wasn't it at least worth a little experimentation?

As unsettling as this college student's question might be, we must not be too quick to condemn him. His thinking is simply a logical progression of our own generation. We have been doing a "little experimentation" with our mores for years. We have substituted "situational morality" for God's unchanging laws.

Shame, blame, compunction, censure, culpability and guilt, it is advised, suppress the individual. Even some churches shy away from mentioning them. We concentrate instead on "positive things," human rights—the "freedom to be me."

I don't mean to sound pious. I have no claim to that. I am as prone to alibi my actions as anyone else. But I think we have to face the facts: our propensity to rationalize good for evil is growing faster now.

"Woe unto them that seek deep to hide their counsel from the Lord," Isaiah cautioned, "and their works are in the dark, and they say, Who seeth us? and who knoweth us? Surely your turning of things upside down shall be esteemed as the potter's clay: for shall the work say of him that made it, He made me not? or shall the thing framed say of him who framed it, He had no understanding?" (Isaiah 29: 15, 16).

But how does the devil get us to do it? How can we be so duped that we are lulled into ignoring the transformation taking place before our eyes, until one day we awaken to find evil smeared everywhere?

In the case of homosexuality, I think, the idea has been so repulsive to our culture, we have tended to ignore it. The problem is, then, when it is suddenly thrust upon us, we have forgotten why it isn't right.

And, frankly, it has some charm about it. Young people who encounter the gay scene for the first time, often mention how wonderful is its pervasive quality of love. There is much physical touching. There is much laughter. There is much concern expressed one for the other.

We all need love. We all need the expression of concern from others, and, in turn, need to express our concern. And in the impersonal concrete and steel megalopoli which scar our landscape from sea to shining sea there is much loneliness.

The initial impression of homosexual society seems to say it offers an alternative to the empty feeling of personal isolation. And there is an evident camaraderie among gays at a very human level (as opposed to a sexual one). But it is the comradeship of the outsider. Many homosexuals have given up jobs, families, friends because of sexual identity. This gives them a common bond.

But if you are around homosexuals very long, you come to realize the veneer is a fragile one, masking the very loneliness it seems to overcome. Even those psychologists, psychotherapists, sociologists and other experts who say there are "happy homosexuals," concede most gays are intensely lonely people.

The reason for this, I think, is because without exception practicing homosexuals are sex obsessed. They place their sexuality before everything else in life; before family, before friends, before God.

The law is plain: "Thou shalt have no other gods before me" (Exodus 20:3).

Without debate, many heterosexuals are guilty of the same sin. Normal sex oft times comes before God. So does materialism, family loyalty, television. We make false gods of many things. It is the turning of things upside down, as Isaiah said.

But we are a nation drunk with sex and knowledge. Is it too late to sober up?

5
Gay Isn't, Is It?

I remember Brice.

Brice was a bright, capable actor who could sing and dance with the best of them. He looked like a younger, thinner version of Tony Curtis, the Hollywood star. As a result, he was often cast as the romantic lead in the stock theatre which employed our talents.

It was reported that he was the only son of an upstate New York godfather who ruled with an iron fist one of the largest "families" in organized crime. And Brice could give a pretty good "tough-guy" performance in real life when he wanted. Unlike the rest of us struggling thespians, he had a lot of money given him by his father which he spent freely. These two attributes alone made him the darling of the "Stagedoor Janes" (A term for the usually older, wealthy women who dote on being seen with handsome young actors.) who came backstage every night in the hope of meeting and dating two or three of the most dashing male members of our company.

They never seemed to be able to figure out why Brice wouldn't give them a tumble. But the theatre folk knew. The only date Brice wanted was with another actor in the cast. The two were very devoted to each other.

Offstage, among his friends, Brice assumed very effeminate mannerisms. He enjoyed entertaining us with his impersonations of the famous actress Tallulah Bankhead. He never donned feminine dress, but he had her movements and voice down pat.

The funny thing was, Brice enjoyed playing "cupid" among his heterosexual friends. He was forever telling me, "What you need is to find a nice girl and settle down and raise lots of kids."

More than any other cast member, Brice respected my Christian background. Whenever I missed church, he would chastise me in no uncertain terms and elicit my promise to be in the front pew the following Sunday.

I used to think Brice was the most likable, well-balanced homosexual I ever had known.

Then Brice had a quarrel with his partner. There was quite a heated exchange and the two broke off their relationship. Almost immediately, Brice began to court the female ingenue. She was the archtype of the "dumb-blonde," about as farm-fresh naive as a girl could ever be.

Most of us speculated that Brice was romancing this girl to make his partner jealous. Homosexuals will often utilize such a ploy. There is no greater insult to a homosexual than to have the object of their intention demonstrate an interest in the opposite sex.

But as Brice's romance with his leading lady went on for much longer than any of us thought it would, there was a great deal of head scratching and wonder among the members of the company.

Then one day, I met Brice on the elevator of the hotel where we were all billeted. The always happy Brice seemed even happier on that afternoon.

"What's got you so elated?" I asked.

"Guess what," he smiled showing his even, white-capped teeth from ear to ear, "I've discovered I'm bisexual. Would you believe it, I'm normal!"

To understand the importance of this announcement, you have to understand that in the gay community, under the influence of Kinsey I suppose, the norm is often considered a state of bisexuality.

"That isn't normal to me," I shot back.

"Please, no sermons today," he said. "I think I'm normal and that's all that counts." And then a faraway look came into his eyes. "Being gay isn't really gay, you know," he said. "Sometimes it's pretty bleak and pretty lonely. You feel so apart from everyone else."

I wish I could write that Brice married the girl who made him feel like he belonged to the human race. But he did not. The last time I saw him in Los Angeles, he was again involved in the homosexual scene. He was genuinely glad that I had at last found the girl of my dreams and that we had a child with another on the way. He was happy, too, I had quit the theatre and had gone into business.

"You were never really cut out for life on the stage," he said. "You had a faith. You didn't need the applause like some of the rest of us. You always knew who you were and what you were."

"Being gay isn't, is it?" I said.

"What do you know about it? Who told you that?"

"You did once—a long time ago," I reminded him.

"Oh," he said. That was all. "Oh." To me, it sounded sad, almost tragic.

We shook hands and went our separate ways.

My wife and I moved away from Southern California shortly afterwards. Every once in awhile, I see Brice on a television show. He has built a fairly successful career playing tough-guy romantic leads. The publicity about him always reports what a nice, happy Hollywood figure he is and the photos always show him smiling. But I think I can see between the lines and behind that unassuming countenance. I think I can see the melancholy loneliness that dwells with the inner man. And I wonder, why do they call them "gay"?

Their lifestyle seems anything but. A Christian psychiatrist has been quoted as saying, "All homosexuals are liars."

In a sense all mankind are liars, so he is not necessarily pointing the finger of prejudice at gays with this provocative indictment. He is, it was explained to me, attempting to dramatize how the gays' sexual preference puts them at odds with society's acceptable standard of behavior. They learn early that public revelation of their condition subjects them to brutal public condemnation and so they have a tendency to hide what they are as much as possible from other people.

Homosexuals learn to practice public deceit so often that, after a time, they cannot distinguish between truth and falsehood in their own private thoughts. And "coming out of the closet" is merely an extension of that self-delusion.

Gays con themselves, believing that if they accept their

sexual abnormality as normal for them, then other people will have to accept it too. They tell themselves that once they "are declared," the terrible secret burden which they carry will be lifted. They tell themselves that they will be happy, really happy for the first time in their lives.

But, "The heart," Jeremiah lamented, "is deceitful above all things, and desperately wicked: who can know it?" (17:9).

Proverbs fills us in on the inevitable outcome of self-delusion: "Bread of deceit is sweet to a man; but afterwards his mouth shall be filled with gravel" (20:17).

First Timothy 4:2 echoes the thought in speaking of those who tell lies "in hypocrisy; having their conscience seared with a hot iron."

If you've ever burned your hand severely, you know that at first such a burn feels almost cool. But then the excruciating pain surges through you in sickening waves, each wave more terrible than the last. The same thing happens to the liar.

At first the lie seems a relief, soothing, almost curative. But the searing anguish of falsehood will eventually sweep through the conscience, burning, burning, BURNING deep into the heart. How does the homosexual, who admits and relishes with pride what he is, deceive himself?

God, through His servant Paul, has said in I Corinthians 11:9, "Neither was the man created for the woman; but the woman for the man." And in verse 11 of the same chapter we read, "Nevertheless neither is the man without the woman, neither the woman without the man, in the Lord."

Genesis 2:24 sheds more light on the matter: "Therefore shall a man leave his father and his mother, and shall cleave unto his wife: and they shall be one flesh."

The concept of "one flesh" in God's constructed creation is a vital one to our inner feeling of well-being. It is far more than a sexual completion of man and woman. It is the wedding of the two highest elements of God's universal order into one whole. It is the divine joining of mind and soul—and all the diverse components implied by these two words—into the perfect totality of life. I believe the instinct for such completion exists in every individual. It is as basic to the human species as hibernation is to bears or spawning is to salmon.

But can the homosexual satisfy that instinct of union with another of the same sex? God has pointed the way in the physical world. You cannot have an electrical current without both positive and negative electrons. The smallest particle of any element—the atom—would not be, without positive and negative attraction. Remove opposites and the physical world would self-destruct in milli-seconds.

So, opposites are essential in the state of total human fulfillment as well. As with the heterosexual so with the homosexual, the instinct for completion dwells within us all. No amount of surface self-deceit can eliminate this innate force concealed within our subconscious entity.

No surrogate of the same sex can every fully satisfy a person's instinct to complete God's implanted need. No surrogate of the same sex, regardless of how erotically appealing he or she may be, can fully fill the requisite destined by our Maker. Two positives or two minuses do not a current make.

And so the homosexual is doomed to keep searching for the very element perverted desire cannot supply. He may deny it vehemently. He may fool himself. But the instinct is there and I suspect it accounts for the loneliness associated so commonly with the homosexual state.

Of course, there are records of long term homosexual relationships. There is no doubt two gays can display a magnificent devotion to each other quite apart from the sexual aspect. Experts agree that such relationships are more common among women than men. But they are probably the exception even with the female of the species.

Estimates of the rate of promiscuity among homosexual couples range upward to two-thirds of that found in heterosexual couples of the same age and cultural backgrounds. At least one expert says the incidence of promiscuous behavior among gay couples is a flat one hundred percent.

On the other hand, I know of two homosexual people who have appeared to live together year-after-year without unfaithfulness on the part of either partner. Yet, those who know them best say this couple is more asexual than homosexual.

Yes, given the plan of creation, the gays are truly doomed. To seek and never wholly find, to quest and not discover. They search on street corners, in public restrooms, within gay organizations and in bars.

There are an estimated four thousand homosexual bars in the U.S. at this writing. In one city of half a million people, there are an incredible eighteen liquor dispensing hangouts for male homosexuals and two for female homosexuals.

It follows that the rate of alcoholism among gays is much higher than for the normal population. That is why there is a chapter of Alcoholics Anonymous exclusively for their kind.

And because of their promiscuous lifestyle, homosexuals are often lured to out-of-the-way locations to be robbed and beaten. Some are murdered.

Why do they call them "gay"? How did such an antithesis of terminology get attached to sexual inversion?

It wasn't so very long ago that "gay" was not affixed to homosexuality in the communal mind. It was the equivalent of "merry," "bright and lively," "delight," "joyful," "glad," and "splendid."

Remember when "our hearts were young and gay"? That meant we were youthful and merry. A "gay blade" was a ladies' man! The "gay caballero" was an unattached Mexican cowboy who could jump on his horse and head happily for parts unknown without a care. A "gay party" was merely a festive one.

Apply the "gay" adjective to any of the above now, and you immediately have said the person or the situation described has something to do with homosexuals.

"Queer" is another word which has been sullied for the rest of us by association with homosexuals. Queer once meant "odd" or "sick and faint." There was no sexual connotation. A "queer gentleman" was an eccentric one. To say that something was "mighty queer" was to say it was strange and unusual in the course of events.

My grandfather used to say, "I feel mighty queer this morning," meaning he felt a little sickly; had a few aches and pains. If he were alive today and said that, people would talk.

No, "queer" is no longer the harmless, innocent term it once was. It has become a derogatory vulgarism. In fairness, even the gays deplore its homosexual usage. They do not choose it for themselves.

But they *have* chosen "gay." How? Why?

One version has it that "gay" was applied to homosexuals in the theatre as early as the 1700s. There is no record of the reason of the application. It has been suggested it was due to the "sportive" nature of the homophiles it described.

The *Dictionary of American Slang,* compiled by Wentworth and Flexner, seems to infer that it is in some way associated with "gay-cat," sometimes used in speaking of a homosexual jazz musician.

Still a third version gives credit to the American expatriot, Gertrude Stein who was a celebrated lesbian, for importing it to English usage from French.

Whatever is the case, homosexuals themselves have adopted it with fervor. They say it gives a homosexual a positive feeling about himself. The press has been quick to aid and abet their linguistic cause. So now we have "gay rights," "gay pride," "gay parades," and "gay bars."

The truth is that homosexuals as a social class are no more "merry," "glad," or "joyful" than the rest of us. On the strength of the evidence, they are a lot less so.

No matter. "Gay" firmly belongs to them. And they call the rest of us "straight." Straight was originally an antonym for "crooked." It is a compliment. If you are "straight" you are "honest" and "normal."

Or are you?

"Straight" is used in the same sense by both the homosexuals and narcotics users in our society, and has been since the mid-forties. In doing research for a youth program on the dangers of hard drugs for a local police department, I interviewed several addicts who explained that "straight" had another interpretation.

To say that a person was "straight" meant he was "square," not hip, but dull, boorish, a dud, stupid, a clod. Could it be that when homosexuals refer to us as "straight," they really have this second definition in mind? Could it be that they are really insulting us instead of praising us?

Well, I'd rather be "straight" and "square" than "hip" and "gay." If that makes me narrow-minded, I offer no apologies. I take solace in the fact that the Bible says, "Because strait is the gate, and narrow is the way, which leadeth unto life, and few there be that find it" (Matthew 7:14).

Of course, "strait" and "straight" are not quite the same. "Strait" is "compressed," "restricted." "straight" in the dictionary sense is "invariable in direction." But you cannot get through the "strait" without being "straight."

That doesn't sound dull and boring to me. That's a challenge.

Let them call themselves "gay." But...

I remember Brice.

6
None Dare
Call Them Strange

"I've spent years of looking into it [homosexuality] because it affects me directly. I know for a fact...the experts agree... your sexual preference is set by age five...

"Let's accept the reality of homosexuality. It is a reality. Let's not fool ourselves. Your fear and hatred is based out of ignorance 'cause where have you ever heard of homosexuality in a legitimate educational setting?...Let's get it out in the open and look at it for what it is...

"We [homosexuals and heterosexuals] should coexist together without hating each other...

"I don't want you to like me. I just want you to get out of my way. I'm an American citizen. I want my human and civil rights 'cause I'm not bothering you, so I don't want you bothering me...What are you gonna' do, kill us? Then what are you going to do next?...

"You are our problem. You are our problem. I have no problems. You're the problem...

"Why don't you try the gay way? You might like it...You're the sick one [heterosexual]. You're the one preaching hate, not us [the gays]...Just relax and try to think this thing through ...I have never had a gay teacher. I have never read anything about homosexuals while I was in school... I was raised by heterosexual parents. Everything I was ever taught was to be straight. Yet, internally—whatever the causes are—I am gay. No, that's a fact of life. My mother never in her wildest dreams thought I could be gay, just like you in your wildest dreams never think your children or any of your nieces and nephews could be gay. But statistics say ten percent of children will be gay. Now, are you saying those children should never grow up to have a decent job...That's exactly what the issue

51

is. The reality of these gay children...What do you think they should do with the rest of their lives? What would you have us to do with them?...

"It's just plain gut prejudice. Ignorance, too. It's fear [of homosexuals]... It may be fear of one's self, too. Your fear of your own motives, and you wonder what you're doing and you're over-compensating for this fear. What exactly is it you don't agree with?...

"I'll tell you what. If you change the laws tomorrow in this land...and you make it as equal for gay people as it is for anyone else in this land, I'll quit and you'll never hear from me again. But as long as there's oppression, buddy, you're gonna' hear from me and I'm gonna' keep on fightin'...I'm fightin' awful hard... What do you think I am?... Are you saying it [homosexuality] is not right for you?... You have no desire for it, right?... But we do, so do you think for that reason we should be denied our desires and everything?...

"At one time in this country, society didn't agree that blacks were equal...And they should play a subordinate role in life and they should be slaves. It took us what? Two hundred years to come around to realize that blacks are American citizens and human beings...And the ignorance in this area [homosexuality] is based on the same prejudice, this knowledge, this lack of information...

"I have two arms, two legs, two eyes. I'm a man, what more do you want? I like chocolate ice cream over vanilla ice cream...

"Religion is what has caused all the hatred... The whole thing is 'save our children'... Save the Christian schools from these 'horrible' people... I think it sounds ridiculous... Whatever the cause [of homosexuality] is, is irrelevant when you're talking about human rights...

"People like you are punishing the gay children, making them feel less than human...Why do we [the gays] have to keep quiet?...

"Were you ever seen in public with a woman... holding hands?... The point is, you're not hiding the fact you're attracted by women, that you're married to a woman, so why should we have to hide? It's a reality. Why can't we live with

52

it?...

"We don't know why you're the way you are either [why you're heterosexual]... The one fact we're dealing with is that we're homosexuals... Gay men, gay women and gay children ...And whatever the cause of our being gay, we're entitled to our American Constitutional rights. It's that simple... Inasmuch as we're denied our civil rights and not allowed to get jobs, we're a little bit different... We're a minority also, we're not the majority...

"Yes... The black behavior annoys the majority of whites in this country... What was all the sixties about—black behavior and fighting for civil rights. I'm being very frank with you... It [gayness] is natural behavior... The idea is natural... I never chose this life style. It's natural... They cannot turn around a person's sexual behavior...

"I'm sure if many white racists in this country had their way, there would be no blacks in this country, too, because they consider their behavior just as abhorrent as ours [the gays]...

"Who are you to decide what I should be? You may not like me, but what right do you have to force me to change? Who put you in charge? Why can't I say that your [heterosexual] behavior is abhorrent to me?... I am what I am, you are what you are, why can't we get along with one another?...

"What amazes me... everyone that opposes us... says 'change, change, change.' Be like us... As a matter of fact, many men and women that have been forced into the situation [of marriage] by social pressures are, indeed, gay... And the American Association of Psychiatrists said it was not an 'illness'...

"The rights are not yours to give. They're ours as citizens of this country. And just because you don't like us, doesn't mean you can deny us those rights...

"All the [school] teacher can influence is whether [gay children] like themselves or hate themselves...

"Instead of using blacks now, they're using gays... Keep that [your moral objection to homosexuality] in your church and that will be nice...

"It's none of your business. It's none of your business what my body's made for...Just leave me alone!... [Homosexuality] is not right for you, it's right for me, and it's *probably* not right for heterosexual people...

"In the gay world, I know of almost no derogatory words we have for straight people... Would you like us to come up with really negative words? We got 'em. We can call you 'breeders.' Want to be called a 'breeder'?... We can be nasty, but we don't want to be nasty... We are being hated and fired and abused for what we are... We are bothering no one, just having our own fun...

"In Nazi Germany Hitler sought out the gays just like he sought out the Jews. Two-hundred, fifty-thousand gay people were executed. In the McCarthy era—if you know your American history—there were massive witch-hunts trying to find gay people. So don't act like we're yelling loud just for something to do. We're yelling loud to save our lives, to save our jobs...

"You are a Christian-racist bigot!... Christian prejudice astounds me... Your hypocrisy is amazing... You have no need to be afraid of me, to condemn me, except your Bible says homosexuality is a sin... That's just another myth... One of many myths in the Bible. Thinking people are too smart for that anymore... That kind of thinking went out with kerosine lamps... Maybe you're gay, too. Maybe you just don't want other people to know that... You protest too loudly... You're just your normal Christian bigot... You say your God tells you to love people... Well, that's all I do, is love people... That makes me a better Christian than you are according to your own religion... So, just take all your false religious hangups and go crawl off somewhere and let me alone... I mean you no harm. I don't even care about you or what you think... Your mind is too small and brittle for enlightened people... All we want is our human rights."

This rather convoluted argument is virtually a verbatim transcript of remarks made by two homosexuals in a debate with heterosexuals over the subject of gayness. Obviously, I have edited and condensed these statements. But the text remains faithful to the actual spoken dialogue and to the sequence of the discourse.

The heterosexual side of the discussion has been eliminated here because it really makes no difference what those opposed to gayness say, not to the firmly established proponents of perversion at any rate. The pattern of logic posed by the Gay Liberationists is almost the same. It has been carefully designed and scripted to accomplish their objectives: to win sympathy, tolerance and even public support for homosexuality while shaming and shouting the critics into silence.

And the Gay Libbers have the platform now. Their rantings and ravings and bold protestations have made homosexuality news.

Look at what happened in Dade County, Florida, when Anita Bryant addressed the county commissioners as a private citizen. The commissioners passed an ordinance which banned discrimination of any kind against homosexuals. Miss Bryant, a singer, actress and commercial spokeswoman, gave her testimony not as any of these things, but as a private citizen, Mrs. Robert Green, a mother, voicing her opinion on a local issue.

Suddenly, the spotlight of the world was focused upon her for her remarks. A devout, born-again Christian, Miss Bryant had written a number of books concerning her Christian beliefs and principles. These perhaps had been little noted outside evangelical circles although they were fine, inspirational works.

But her objections to the gay ordinance of Dade County became an instant international cause celebre for homosexuals everywhere. They howled long and loud in "righteous" indignation over their "civil rights." They wrote letters of protest to those companies which employed Miss Bryant's services in their advertising. They succeeded in getting one such company to cancel their sponsorship of the singer's new television series. They questioned her motivation, slandered her reputation and abused her intelligence.

Eventually, the company which withdrew its money for her television endeavor, reinstated its sponsorship subject to approval of certain "contract terms." But the startling fact is that the supposed minority of homosexuals in America's midst had been able to pressure such a cancellation in the first place.

It is to Miss Bryant's great credit that she did not fall silent in the face of such brutal tactics. She continued to state her basic objections to the Dade ordinance. Basically, she said—and many religious and civil leaders confirmed her statements—that under the law, private and parochial schools will be forced to hire homosexuals in teaching positions.

Homosexuals immediately denied that this will be the effect of the ordinance. It all has to do with the right to work, they said. One homosexual said over a radio program heard in thirty-eight states that Miss Bryant's understanding of the document was totally erroneous. He said his credentials for making this judgment were that he had recently visited the state of Florida for a few days and had first-hand knowledge. Of course, this bit of rationality completely overlooked the fact that Miss Bryant lived in Dade County with her husband and four children, and thus by this gay's own reasoning should be more knowledgeable on the content and intent of the law than he.

And whether the Dade County ordinance would or would not force the employment of homosexuals in private and parochial institutions remains debatable. But Miss Bryant and her group, Save Our Children, believe the possibility was certain enough that they worked long and hard to gather enough signatures on petitions to force a countywide referendum.

The threat, as Miss Bryant and others see it, is the chance homosexual teachers will "recruit" students to their lifestyle. "Homosexuals cannot reproduce," Miss Bryant said, "so they must recruit."

Homosexuals openly scoff at this, calling it an "irrational fear." "You can't make a homosexual from a straight person," they laugh, "he is either that way to begin with or he isn't. We don't solicit. Never."

If that is so, why have gays viewed the Dade County referendum on the job-discrimination ordinance "a turning point in the gay rights movement"?

This is so critically important to the gay movement that a newspaper wire service reported a San Francisco homosexual leader saying, "If gay people win, it will push us ahead tremendously."

He said it was purely an issue of civil rights. However, the same individual praised boycott efforts against Florida orange juice for which Anita Bryant made a number of commercials and said the boycott would continue, "either until the industry terminates her employment or she stops doing what she's doing, talking hate."

In other words, the very people who posture that gayness is not a case of moral right or wrong, but one of civil rights, are willing to actively work to deny someone else's civil rights.

Contradictory? Incongruous? But a potentially effective technique.

Gay activists bank on the fact that most of society is so put off by homosexuality that people cannot bring themselves to thoroughly investigate the available data. And they are right. It gives the gays a big advantage.

That's why when a heterosexual rises to debate a homosexual, the latter usually begins with a statement like the one which opened this chapter, "I've spent years of looking into it [homosexuality] because it affects me directly...."

The homosexual knows the argument will establish him [or her] as an expert. He knows people will nod their heads in agreement, repeating to themselves, "right. Who should know better about it than he who is?" It makes sense. But the fallacy is, the homosexual's research has probably been extremely biased. He doesn't want to know the negatives about his condition. He wants only the positives. He wants self-justification, the same thing we all want for our actions. Bias isn't a homosexual trait, it's a people trait. Realization of this should cast some doubt on the validity of the homosexual's claim of intellectual expertness.

The Bible, in Galatians 6:3, alerts us to this faulty kind of human self-justification thusly, "If a man think himself to be something, when he is nothing, he deceiveth himself."

Proverbs recognizes it with, "Most men will proclaim every one his own goodness..." (20:6a).

The lesson is clear. See and know such self-proclamation for what it is. For once the gay has established authority, he then launches into a recitation of "proven scientific realities" about homosexuality. The latest of these is, "the tendency to become gay is fixed by the time a child reaches three or four years of age."

Our culture puts a great deal of credence in science. And science has brought us far in the last one hundred years. My own grandparents took a stagecoach to reach their honeymoon retreat. They have lived to see men walk on the moon and to view photographs from Mars. As the slogan of a major corporation used to put it, "Better living through science." And another slogan went, "Progress is our most important project."

We have witnessed so many fantastic advances in our lifetime that in our cultural consciousness we have come to believe science deals in absolutes.

But the nature of science falls short of this definition. Science accumulates observations and experimentations to arrive at its conclusions. The essence of science is the experiment, the test.

I had a high school science teacher who taught, "Science is testing. It helps us arrive at knowledge, but then that knowledge must be tested again and again and again. So, the only scientific certainty is experimentation.

"If I tell you something as fact," he would go on, "test my assertion. If your test tells you I'm right, test your test.

"I am going to teach you some scientific absolutes. I will expect you to repeat them as absolutes on your exam papers, but know that the only thing absolute about them is that they will probably be proven wrong in the next twenty-five years."

That is the history of science. People once thought the sun revolved around the earth. They were wrong.

Scientists once thought the only way to get a rocket to the moon was to build a space station near earth first. They were wrong.

Scientists said that cyclamates caused cancer. That led to a ban on their use in the United States. Now, they have some doubt about it.

The behavioral sciences are even less exact. As we have seen, it was once said that homosexuality was caused by a domineering mother. Today, hardly any behaviorists still hold to that view.

About the only certain thing we really know about homosexuality is that it exists. And the only absolute we can be certain of is that God says it is sin. Beyond that, nothing.

And the statistics quoted in its behalf are just as unreliable. The ten percent figure so often given as the number of homosexuals in society is not at all certain. There may be less, but more probably we are told, there are a lot more.

"Statistically, then," I've heard a homosexual say, "two out of every ten children is a homosexual. If you have five kids, one will probably be a homosexual." That's just playing with numbers.

But the homosexuals have placed much emphasis on just such numbers in recent years. Coupled with that most recent theory of gayness being established by age three or four, they can be a most powerful persuader for support from the heterosexual populace.

The propaganda goes something like this, "All the gays I [the homosexual] know were raised by heterosexual parents like you. They didn't know their kids were gay. They didn't teach their kids to be gay, but they are gay. Now medical doctors know that homosexuality is set by the time a kid is three or four years of age. Two out of every ten kids will grow up homosexual. You don't even know it, but your child could be gay right now. Would you deny him or her? Would you deny him a good job, a good life, security? We don't have to recruit your kid. He's already that way. So when you condemn me, lady, you're really condemning your child."

The argument is designed to go to the heart of those ideals espoused by groups like Anita Bryant's Save Our Children. "What are you saving them from?" it asks. "Themselves? No. You are destroying them by denying them from being themselves." What parent of permissiveness could fail to respond with deep emotion? Few.

After listening to a similar discourse, one father was heard to remark, "I'm telling my boys that homosexuality is not right for me. But, if it suits them, it's okay."

It may be trite, but it is worth repeating and remembering, the Bible says, "Train up a child in the way he should go: and when he is old, he will not depart from it" (Proverbs 22:6). No better advice was ever given.

If you do remember and follow it, if you do not respond to the gays' appeal to your parental instinct, they have other means of dealing with you.

Americans are famous for their desire to be fair to all. We have a sense of "justice" and "fair play" which has grown stronger over the more than two centuries of our existence as a people. We will tolerate anything as long as it is in the name of "liberty" and "freedom."

Knowing this, the gays move to have you class them with all underprivileged peoples. They say they are like the blacks and the chicanos. Americans are still very much aware of the racial strife of the sixties. It is something we all understand to greater or lesser degrees.

As a normal black man or brown man or black woman or brown woman I would be outraged. Homosexuals are not a race. They are not set apart by color, or appearance or language or physical characteristics. They are not a race, they are an aberration. They are of all peoples. Their separation is not of biology in the racial sense, it is a separation in the abnormal sense.

Remind them of this and they will call you a "racist." They will class you with Hitler and Joe McCarthy. And while those charges may seem ridiculous and have no effect on you, they can have a large effect on students and liberals to whom "racist" is a most horrible insult. They do not want to be associated with "racists."

And if you then say your aversion to homosexuality is based upon your religion, the gays will counter with the cry of "bigot." Now, a bigot is one "who is blindly and obstinately devoted to a faith or creed." If in labeling me a bigot, they mean I am blindly devoted to my Lord and Saviour, Jesus Christ, they are correct. But if they mean I am blindly against homosexuality, they are wrong. In Christ I am as the ex-blind man before the judges who said, "...whereas I was blind, now I see" (John 9:25b).

Belief in Jesus Christ opens our eyes to the many sins around us and through us. I see homosexuality for what it is. And I stand against it, not out of fear of punishment by God, but out of love for my Saviour. For He has said unto those who believe, "If ye love me, keep my commandments" (John 14:15).

Granted, there are many who do not accept the Word of God as the final authority. And that is hard for the Christian to accept. We have a tendency to argue first from the Bible, and that is good. The problem is there are so many abroad who will not receive the Scriptures. Jesus encountered them too: "For this people's heart is waxed gross, and their ears are dull of hearing, and their eyes they have closed; lest at any time they should see with their eyes and hear with their ears, and should understand with their heart, and should be converted, and I should heal them" (Matthew 13:15).

Jesus spoke to such people in parables. He spoke to them in the language and in a manner that they could absorb without prejudice. We Christians would do well to follow the Master's example when debating with homosexuals and their supporters. "By long forbearing is a prince persuaded, and a soft tongue breaketh the bone" (Proverbs 25:15).

Well, if they can't persuade you through science and statistics; if they can't silence you by calling you a "racist religious bigot," they will resort to the most obscene epithet of all.

Witness this written statement by one of the psychologists who defends homosexuality: "Why should anything as unobtrusive as homosexuality arouse as much concern as it does? On the surface there seem to be as many answers as there are critics, critics who sometimes feel the urge to defend the church, the home, society in general, or their own backyards. There are . . . always the most vociferous of the lot, who want to smite the homosexual dragon from without to keep from seeing it within."

He is saying, if you cry too long and too loud, you—despite your confessed aversion to homosexuality—are really gay. It's a common ploy.

Personally, I am not a critic of the current Gay Invasion because I want to defend the church. The true church, the Body of Christ, needs no defense. My home and my backyard need no protection, because Christ has been invited into them. Society in general will not be defended. But it is for those who are weak in Christ for whom I speak.

I find inspiration in the speech Paul made to the elders of the church at Ephesus. It was at the close of his third missionary journey. He knew that he would probably never see these people again in this life, so what he said had to count. Here's just a part of his text on that occasion:

"But none of these things move me, neither count I my life dear unto myself, so that I might finish my course with joy, and the ministry, which I have received of the Lord Jesus, to testify the gospel of the grace of God.

"...Take heed therefore unto yourselves, and to all the flock, over the which the Holy Ghost hath made you overseers, to feed the church of God, which he hath purchased with his own blood. For I know this, that after my departing shall grievous wolves enter in among you, not sparing the flock.

"Also of your own selves shall men arise, speaking perverse things to draw away disciples after them. Therefore watch, and remember, that by the space of three years I ceased not to warn every one night and day with tears" (Acts 20:24, 28-31).

The church needs no defense. But it does need to be fed on truth and light. So, in a very real sense, we are waiters, servants. We don't design the menu, we don't prepare the food, but we must serve it where ordered.

My initial impulse when someone says I want "to smite the homosexual dragon from without to keep from seeing it within" is to rearrange his similes and metaphors for him. But St. George himself could not kill the ghost of doubt raised by these critics. If accuse me of that he will, let him accuse. Those who are wont to believe in the gossip will, and no violence or protestations will deter them.

But neither will the accusations silence me, nor should they be allowed to silence any other person speaking against homosexuality. If we fall silent, we give authenticity to the slander and the libel.

Doubt is what they hope to raise, not only doubt about them, but doubt about ourselves as well.

Our bachelor uncles are no longer just eccentric or too finicky for marriage as we once thought they were. You don't suppose...?

Two men who share living quarters no longer do so just to cut housing expenses, do they? You don't suppose...?

And the football players and the business men who pat others on the back for a job well-done, you don't suppose...?

And the two women seen walking through the park arm-in-arm wouldn't do that to steady one another, would they? You don't suppose...?

And the Hollywood star who is a little too handsome or a little too pretty, you don't suppose...?

And the television comic who seems a little effeminate, that isn't just his style, is it?

And the man or woman who treats their mother with kindness when over twenty, you don't suppose...?

See how the doubts feed and build on one another?

There is another kind of doubt gays deliberately foster. We have heard for years that homosexuals never approach heterosexuals. They are supposed to have some sort of "built-in radar" which helps them to identify other gays through ESP. They make advances only toward people who are already gay.

If that is true, why then do homosexuals display certain signals to be seen by other gays? Male homosexuals in the nineteenth and early twentieth century in New York City used to wear red neckties so that other gays would know who they were. Why once did they affect a single earring? When I was in college, homosexuals were said to be those who wore green on Thursday. Pity the heterosexual fellow who wore green by accident on the fifth day of the week.

Prior to recent development in educational circles, homosexuals freely admitted that they did recruit. A book by two homosexuals published in 1972, stated that the practice should be no more offensive to the propositioned heterosexual than if he had been asked by a member of the opposite sex. After all, the authors reasoned, the heterosexual so approached by a gay could always answer with a "firm no."

But what about the homosexual who does not take "no" for

an answer? What about the young and the uninitiated and the weak of will who do not know how to be firm in their rejection of other people?

When a homosexual says, "I want you," he is not operating with ESP or radar or any special inate intuition. Homosexuals do recruit heterosexuals both by mistake and design, and especially in a society or subculture where being "found out" carries no serious consequences.

The theatre is that kind of subculture. I have seen heterosexuals propositioned by homosexuals because the gays had nothing to lose and everything to gain. There was one girl who broke up with her boy friend. Tabby, a lesbian, consoled the girl and before long was obviously her lover.

"But the girl must have been homosexual and didn't know it," is the argument. Yeah? What about Sam?

Sam was eighteen, in his freshman year. He had quite a black book filled with the names and phone numbers of some of the best looking girls on campus. And then Sam was approached by Biff.

It shook Sam. It filled him with doubt. "Maybe I am gay. They don't approach people who aren't. Maybe he sees something about me I don't know yet," Sam said.

No way. In the animal kingdom when too many male rats are placed together, the society becomes homosexual. The homosexual rats attack heterosexual rats, and pretty soon, the attacked become as gay as the others. This has been observed in the laboratory.

But the very Gay Libbers who sometimes point to the animal world to prove that homosexuality is a natural thing, spurn as "invalid" the experiments with rats. You can't apply rat behavior to human behavior, they say. Could it be that gays are as hypocritical as heterosexuals?

They are just as human as the rest of us, aren't they? And absolutely more militant than we are anymore. It is ironic that passivity was once believed to be the hallmark of the homosexual while aggressiveness was the trademark of the heterosexual.

We have changed and we are confused. Tell a homosexual

he is different and outside the mainstream of American sexual thought and he may sue you. Tell him he's abnormal and he will campaign to have you lose your job. Tell him his act offends you and he will tell you it's none of your business. Tell him to leave your children alone and he will tell you your children are already gay and you are too dumb to know it. Tell him he cannot teach your children and he will tell you that you are denying your children a "positive role-model."

He can impugn your integrity, challenge your sexuality and offend your intelligence and if you so much as lift a whimper of protest, he says it is you who have violated his civil rights.

Increasingly, the critic of homosexual lifestyle pays a high price for the privilege of speaking his mind and heart. The homosexuals want it that way. They don't want the other side to be heard. They want their truth and only their version of the truth abroad in the land.

That's why they campaign so hard to make sure that none dare to call them strange.

7
Were David and Jonathan "That Way" Too?

Oh, how I wish I could go back to the Cottage.

The Cottage was the greasy spoon cafe just across the street from the theatre building at the university I attended. Mel, the guy who ran it along with his father, learned to cook while he was in the Navy. At least, that was what he said. Those who partook of the Cottage fare doubted that Mel had ever learned to cook at all.

And whatever else the Navy had taught Mel, it had not given him any lasting reverence for the well-known naval tradition of cleanliness. I don't think the bilious green walls of the place had been painted since Mel's father first opened the doors forty years before. Greasy dirt covered everything, including the menus.

They were torn and tattered, mere shadows of their former selves. They were at least twenty years old at that time. Mel had never changed anything anyway, except the prices. When he did that, he'd cross out the present price and pen in the new one. There were so many crossed-out prices on those menus that trying to figure out what something cost was like working an advanced problem in calculus.

The Cottage had a single waitress, Ruth. Ruth was singular in more ways than one. She only had one good arm. The other was crippled and twisted and totally useless. But she didn't let that stop her. She could handle more dishes and cups with her good arm than most waitresses can balance with two. And she had a heart of gold, because whenever she placed one of Mel's concoctions in front of you she would always whisper, "I wouldn't eat that if I were you."

As I write this, I realize how outrageous it sounds. But so help me, the Cottage was really like that. I say "was" because it was torn down several years ago to make room for the university expansion. They say Mel made a lot of money from the sale of the land on which the Cottage stood and moved to California and purchased a very elegant restaurant and hired a French chef to do the cooking for him.

But in those days, Mel did all the cooking himself, and that certainly wasn't a recommendation for the squeamish or faint-hearted. What drew us to the place was not the quality of the food. It was the quantity and the price. For whatever else the Cottage was, it was cheap and Mel was tolerant of student ways.

The price of a single cup of coffee or a rancid glass of iced tea would rent you table space by the hour. And refills were free.

The clientele was a diverse group: students from every discipline—the physical sciences, the behavioral sciences, some theology students from the liberal seminary which shared the campus and, of course, theatre majors. As a result, on any afternoon, the Cottage was filled with the echoes of the kind of deep philosophical discussions of which fledgling collegiate eggheads are so fond.

I'll never forget one discussion that took place over the cracked plastic top of a Cottage table. It was between a theology student, a graduate student in psychology named Russell (no one ever called him 'Russ'), a couple of undergraduates and myself.

Russell was holding forth on the subject of abnormal psychology and eventually he got around to homosexuality. He was arguing that it had been a widely subscribed to practice all down through history. I was attempting to refute his arguments with what was then a pretty meager knowledge of what the Bible had to say on the subject.

"Levitical law may have condemned it," he hissed in my direction with obvious disdain, "but at the same time the Bible gives an excellent and positive example of episodic homosexuality. And it does it without one word of condemnation."

I gave him an "I-don't-believe-it" look.

"It's quite true," he insisted. "David and Jonathan were that way, you know.

I didn't know and told him as much. My father was a native Missourian and I had inherited a lot of that old Missouri "Show me" attitude. And that's exactly what Russell proceeded to do. Borrowing a Bible from the theology student and using the Scriptures he made a most convincing case for his contention.

Since that time I have read the same argument in several books, but that day I was hearing it for the first time. I must admit, it sounded plausible then and can seem even more plausible when you encounter it on the printed page. But, as Russell finished, I knew the Scripture had been abused. I felt it, but didn't know why. Only had I known then what I know now.

The epic of David and Jonathan begins with I Samuel 18. David had slain Goliath, an act of heroism which inspired the Hebrew army to route the Philistines. Saul inquired of his servants as to the identity of the young warrior. When they couldn't tell him who the boy was, Saul called David into his presence and questioned him.

What an impression David must have made, for when the conference was finished, ". . . the soul of Jonathan [Saul's son and heir] was knit with the soul of David, and Jonathan loved him as his own soul" (I Samuel 18:1). In verse 3 of the same chapter we read, "Then Jonathan and David made a covenant, because he loved him as his own soul."

"See?" the discoursers say, "we are given a hint that the relationship between David and Jonathan was one of pederasty." That is a sexual relationship in which an older man is sexually attracted to a young boy.

But it was not. It was a friendship of the best and highest kind. The Bible tells us "the Lord was with" David (I Samuel 18:12). Would God have blessed him if he had been engaged in the unrepentant practice of an act which the Lord had labeled a sin? God had prescribed death for that sin. And, we must remember, He displayed no hesitancy in punishing David for his sin with Bathsheba a few years later.

"Ah, but wait," the authors of deceit urge. "There's more."

David became a great leader among the Israelites, praised and adored by the masses. Saul, in a none too stable mental condition, contrived to undo the upstart from Bethlehem. He attempted to murder David.

Failing, he then tried to use the promise of marriage to his oldest daughter, Merab, to force David into rashly putting his life on the line in battle with the Philistines (I Samuel 18:25).

When that plan went awry, too, Saul married Merab to another man to spite David, giving him a second daughter, Michal for wife. Apparently, Saul felt Michal would do whatever he decreed and, thus, be the perfect spy and betrayer of her new husband, for when Michal fell in love with David, Saul was the more fearful of the popular young shepherd.

So it was, King Saul called a meeting and goaded his aides and his son, Jonathan, to kill David. "But Jonathan...delighted much in David," I Samuel 19:2 says, and refused to do his father's bidding.

"Delighted," the opportunistic intellectuals smirk in repetition, as if that word was supposed to have some sexual implication. Actually, it simply means that Jonathan, along with most of the rest of Israel, was highly pleased with the youthful hero.

Denied Jonathan's help, Saul continued his vendetta. He again tried to impale David with a javelin. And when David escaped that, Saul next tried to take David in David's own house. But Michal helped her husband to flee before Saul arrived with his henchmen.

Saul and his men followed David in his flight, but David managed to elude them and returned to confront Jonathan. As described in I Samuel 20, David begs his friend to explain just what it is that he, David, has done to earn Saul's wrath. Why, David begs, does Saul seek his life?

Jonathan cannot believe that Saul still wants to slay David. He says it is impossible, his father would do nothing without consulting with him. Jonathan and Saul had no secrets from each other, or so Jonathan thought.

But David tried to show Jonathan that Saul had a motive for keeping the latest plot secret from his son. The reason being that Saul knew what good friends David and Jonathan had become. "Thy father," David argued, "certainly knoweth that

I have found grace in thine eyes. . ." (I Samuel 20:3).

"Grace" is another of the words which are deemed fraught with homosexual suggestiveness by the intemperate interpreters. In context here, however, it can only be transcribed by a series of nouns to glean all its overtones. Among these are "favor," "friendship," "loyalty" and "allegiance." To put David's statement in a modern context, one might render it something like this: "He knows we are friends. He's afraid you might warn me, so he's keeping you in the dark."

And, yet, the sexual modernists propose that this is one of at least two passages in Scripture that give us a confession from David's own lips of his homosexual love for Jonathan. The other is found in II Samuel 1:26 as part of David's lament for his friend who had fallen in battle: "I am distressed for thee, my brother Jonathan: very pleasant hast thou been unto me: thy love to me was wonderful, passing the love of women."

What in the world did David mean?

Down through the ages, a certain "mystic" has been observed in sexual relationships. Modern behaviorists have come to realize that this "mystic" is not only conducive to erotic attraction, it is essential. In a way, it is a "gap" created by the different physical and mental characteristics of the male and female. A man thinks and reacts to situations and circumstances differently than a woman and vice versa. Thus, even in the most intimate relationship, the gap between the sexes can never be completely closed and hence the "mystic."

But humankind also has a need for relationships beyond the erotic experience. Psychologists and sociologists classify this need as "the bond of likekind." It is the necessity of sharing a part of a life with an individual who is "likeminded," whose experience and background and station in life are similar and common to yours. We have designated it "friendship," but that designation is wholly inadequate. "Filial love" probably comes closer to the mark.

Because the relationship is so close, there is no gap, no mystic. One prominent psychotherapist says of this bond, "The closeness of it, its likemindedness, and its camaraderie offer too little gap for sex to bridge."

The fulfillment is spiritual as opposed to sexual. It is beyond the realm of the flesh. Friendships like that are extremely rare. If you have experienced just one in your entire lifetime, consider yourself very fortunate.

In the days of David, the differences in the gender roles of men and women were much more pronounced than they are in our culture. Women were kept in harems. They were pampered, they were not considered the intellectual equals of men. The communication between male and female was largely physical. And the close psychic attachment so associated with modern marriage must have been found lacking in a great majority of ancient male-female liaisons. How treasured then, must have been the opportunity of exchanging ideas, concepts and feelings with a likeminded individual. How in those times such closeness of thought must have seemed to surpass the love of a woman.

David's confession, you see, was not the confession of sexual love; it was a confession of filial love.

And Jonathan's motivation for refusing to join his father's conspiracy of murder was loyalty to that friendship.

"But that overlooks Saul's eyewitness description," the intellectuals scoff. They are referring to I Samuel 20:30, "Then Saul's anger was kindled against Jonathan, and he said unto him, Thou son of the perverse rebellious woman, do not I know that thou hast chosen the son of Jesse to thine own confusion, and unto the confusion of thy mother's nakedness?"

It is claimed that Saul's comparison is to uncovering the father's nakedness in Genesis 9:20-25 and a veiled reference to the usual Canaanite debauchery and in that light, clearly talks of a sexual relationship.

Yes, Saul is probably making an accusation of sodomic behavior. But consider the source and the situation. It was a meal at which other people were present: the members of the king's court. Saul, as we have seen, was insanely jealous of David. He wanted to destroy the younger man at any cost. He realized that David had replaced him in the hearts and minds of the citizens of his kingdom, an unforgivable offense to someone possessing the lust for power which Saul possessed.

71

In our day, we have seen many examples of political "dirty tricks," and that is exactly what Saul was playing. From time immemorial, one of the best ways to discredit a political opponent has been to level the charge of "homosexual" against him. It can be so easily and quickly believed by the masses and so stubbornly difficult to disprove and deny.

The best refutation of Saul's unkind lie is Jonathan's reaction to it reported in I Samuel 20:34, "So Jonathan arose from the table in fierce anger, and did eat no meat the second day of the month: for he was grieved for David, because his father had done him shame."

The shame was the slander.

The shame today is the further slander that intellectuals attach to I Samuel 20:41. The scene was the secret meeting wherein Jonathan told David that he must go away to keep from being slain.

The verse says, "David arose out of a place toward the south, and fell on his face to the ground, and bowed himself three times: and they kissed one another, and wept one with another, until David exceeded." The last word in the passage equals "recovered" in modern English.

The act of kissing is said to be homosexual in nature. Ridiculous!

The men of the Mid East and Europe have always been more emotional than their Western counterparts. We used to live down the block from a Greek family. The son of that family and I were "best friends" for a time in high school. I knew them all very well.

A male friend from the old country lived with them for several months. And when he left for the homeland there was much weeping and kissing between the men of the family and their departing guest. No one in their wildest imaginations could have ascribed any homosexual innuendos to what they witnessed. It was the Greek way of saying "good-by." As it was then, so it was in David's day.

It was quite customary in Bible times for men who were close friends to kiss when greeting each other or taking leave one from another. Judas betrayed Christ with a kiss (Matthew

72

26:48, Mark 14:44 and Luke 22:47-48). In his letter to the churches at Rome and at Corinth, Paul admonishes the members, male and female, to greet each other with a consecrated or "holy" kiss (Romans 16:16 and I Corinthians 16:20). So, while we in our culture would be appalled by two unrelated men kissing in public view, all through the centuries in which the Bible was being written, a kiss between friends of the same sex was traditional. To attach any homosexual symbolism to it is to commit the grossest kind of error.

Further, there seems to be some evidence to indicate that David, himself, considered homosexuality a curse. When Joab assassinated Abner, David proclaimed in wrath, "Let it rest on the head of Joab, and on all his father's house; and let there not fail from the house of Joab one that hath an issue, or that is a leper, or that leaneth on a staff, or that falleth on the sword, or that lacketh bread" (II Samuel 3:29).

Some Biblical authorities render the phrase "that leaneth on a staff" as a "distaff holder," meaning unfit for military duty, or "who holds a spindle," which would definitely be an allusion to an effeminate man, since men did not spin or weave.

And why shouldn't David have thought homosexuality was a curse? He was a Jew under the Levitical law. His sin was not homosexuality or bisexuality. The sin for which God punished him was the coveting of his neighbor's wife followed by an attempt to cover up that sin.

Of course, there are those who maintain David would have no knowledge of the Levitical prohibition against sodomy. They say the Scripture we now know as "Leviticus" was not written until the Babylonian Captivity several centuries after David "slept with his fathers."

But the Bible says, "And the Lord spake unto Moses saying..." Those words open the twentieth chapter of Leviticus, the chapter which contains the law against homosexuality. If a choice must be made between the authority of human scholars and the authority of the Bible, the prudent man must choose the Book everytime.

If faith alone was the only means we had of proving the Bible's accuracy, it would be more than sufficient. However,

God has been merciful enough to give us hard evidence that His inspired Word says what it means and means what it says.

In their excellent work, *The Closer You Look The Greater The Book"* (Accent Books), George and Charlotte Syme give instance after instance in which the Bible is supported and proved by the disciplines of science, history and archaeology. One example of which I am the most familiar has to do with the "goof" scholars said existed in Isaiah 20:1. In that verse is found the mention of a "King Sargon." No such monarch was cited in any other ancient source then known.

Isaiah had said Sargon was the king of Assyria. Surely, scholars reasoned, if such a king had lived and ruled over so important a kingdom, other ancient writers would have written reams about him. Some theorized that Isaiah had mistakenly called another Assyrian king by the wrong name. Others said Sargon was only a figment of the prophet's imagination. It really did not matter what the case was, because in either event, it was a glaring error in a Scripture which was supposed to be divinely faultless. Therefore, the scholars said, the Bible was not what it pretended. It was fallible.

For years the argument raged. Then in the middle of the last century, archaeologists excavated a mound in the Middle East and when they got to the bottom of their pit, do you know where they found themselves? In the middle of King Sargon's own throne room. The Bible was exonerated beyond a shadow of a doubt.

There are many, many more examples. The truth is, the Bible has never proved incorrect by science or history. And so, if it says Moses (who lived long before David tended his father's sheep) handed down the Levitical law, it speaks the truth of the ages. There is no room for question. And, even if we suppose the Book was lost or hidden, even if we suppose that David did not have access to the actual written word, he probably knew the law as well as you and I. The Hebrew people have been blessed with an uncanny ability to pass oral traditions verbatim from one generation to the next, until they were finally committed to parchment by a scribe.

Despite all the testimony to the contrary, the story of David and Jonathan is used more widely than ever before to suggest that the Bible condones homosexuality. The theory is taught as truth on college campuses, in books, magazines and in churches of some of the most respected Christian denominations. And it is growing in popularity and acceptance. But it is not the ultimate blasphemy.

The ultimate blasphemy is so bizarre, I hesitate to repeat it here. However, if you have not already encountered it you doubtless will in the near future. A widely distributed Hollywood motion picture has recently presented it as if it were fact. It is the sacrilegious assertion that Jesus of Nazareth was gay!

This insolent bit of intellectual profanity is predicated on the biography of Jesus as given by the Gospel writers. The close relationship which Jesus enjoyed with His mother is pointed out as a good indication of His "tendency toward homosexuality." Three times after He was over thirty she came after Him, and that is, they say, "a tell-tale sign."

Come now. Is a man to stop loving his mother just because he has seen one score and ten? Should he forbid her visit him for fear he will be branded as "that way?" But then, Jesus was unmarried. A bachelor who loves his mother is the worst kind of son, at least in reputation it seems.

And doesn't the Gospel of John talk thrice of "the disciple whom Jesus loved" (John 13:23, 19:26 and 21:7)? And doesn't the Bible say Jesus "loved Lazarus" (John 11:5 and 36)? Yes, Jesus *esteemed* both. He respected them. He set a high value on them as friends. Has the word love become so debauched we can no longer use it without debasing the holy Gospels?

"But a man who ran around the countryside with twelve other men—His disciples—must be considered strange," the impious argue. In the sense that there were none like Him, Jesus was strange. But to suggest that His choice of twelve male followers is evidence of homosexuality is ludicrous. The twelve were representative of the twelve tribes of Israel, a fulfillment of the prophecies concerning the Messiah.

Besides, while the twelve apostles formed the inner circle, the Bible speaks of "the multitudes" who followed Him from place to place (Matthew 4:25 among other references); and we know those multitudes contained women for Matthew 27:55 relates, "And many women were there... which followed Jesus from Galilee..."

The Bible speaks directly to the heart of the issue. It tells us that while Jesus was "tempted in all points... like we are, yet [he was] without sin" (Hebrews 4:15). He was the "Christ, who through the eternal Spirit offered himself without spot to God..." (Hebrews 9:14). He was "a lamb without blemish and without spot..." (I Peter 1:19). He was the One "who did no sin, neither was guile found in his mouth..." (I Peter 2:22). In short, "In him is no sin" (I John 3:5). We know what homosexuality is. According to the Scripture, it could not be in Him.

In justice, there are homosexuals who believe in Jesus Christ and who are as outraged by the profaning of His holy character as any born-again heterosexuals. There are other homosexuals who argue for the tolerance of the gay lifestyle without defaming David or our Saviour.

Dr. Lynn R. Buzzard, a professor of practical theology at Northern Baptist Theological Seminary, has discussed in *Eternity* magazine the law interpreted from points of Christian view: There are some Biblical laws which Christians believe were intended as ceremonial law for the Israelites. There are other laws which Christ displaced and made unnecessary. Another body of laws can be applied only to the specific culture for which they were framed. But certain Old Testament laws are with universal moral meaning and are God's will for all people in all ages.

Dr. Buzzard admits in his article titled "How Gray Is Gay?" that the distinction between the kinds of Biblical law is not always easy to draw. "But," he wrote, "it is clear that when the writers of the Bible talked about homosexuality, they are talking about a moral issue."

Paul is generally credited as the New Testament writer who introduced the Levitical prohibition of homosexuality into Christian literature. His missionary journeys took him into many of the major cities of the Roman Empire.

Rome was debauched. Its senators, its Caesars, its men of

letters, its artists and its poets practiced homosexuality on a grand scale. Nero, the persecutor of the early Christian church, had been so bold as to "marry" an effeminate boy. Paul saw plainly the wickedness around him and he wrote of it frequently.

Detractors of Paul say that he was a zealot for the cause of purity in sexual matters. Paul was no prude. He was a Christian moralist. The two must not be confused. A prude is one who affects a posture of being overly modest. A moralist is a teacher and writer who deals with ethics.

To imply, as modernists do, that Paul's moral instructions in sexual matters are "too Jewish" for Christian consideration in the nineteen-seventies is to miss God's purpose in choosing Saul of Tarsus as His missionary to the Gentiles. There was no better legal mind in all of the Holy Land. Saul knew the law backward and forward. And when he met Christ face-to-face on the Damascus road, when he was transformed from Saul of Tarsus to Paul, his legalistic approach to life was tempered with grace.

Paul was the necessary link to the heathen world of the Gentiles. The Gentiles had no understanding of the law of God. Their societies were built on humanistic and pagan ethics. As the brilliant lawyer he was, Paul was able to separate the ceremonial and cultural laws of the Hebrew code, to single out the laws which Christ supplanted and to identify the great unchanging moral truths which God intended for all of mankind through all of history.

His stand on kosher food, for example, was a daring and bold new interpretation of Levitical code (I Corinthians 8:4-13). Paul did not subscribe to legalism in the Christian church, he preached that Christ had broken that bond. But he did subscribe to the Lord's unbending ethics and, despite the fact that they were saved by grace, he urged Christians—both Jew and Gentile—to observe those ethics throughout their lives.

As Christians, we are not subject to the Old Testament law; Jesus Christ fulfilled the law—He met its demands perfectly and paid its penalties for us (see Romans 8:2-4). But we are as much under God's unchanging moral law as were the children of Israel in the wilderness. Thus, the Levitical prohibition against homosexuality does apply to today's church and today's Christians.

But do women come under the law against homosexuality? The language in Leviticus is couched in male terms. It mentions only men with men, not women with women. Other personal prohibitions plainly spell out that they are for both sexes but not homosexual acts. You will hear it said sometimes that women, therefore, are free to practice lesbianism without compunction. One author stated the case like this, "It is remarkable that while both men and women are warned against the practice of bestiality, no reference at all is made to female homosexuality in the Levitical law, nor anywhere else in the Bible."

Can it be that Scripture is silent on female homosexuality?

Think of the law in terms of Old Testament customs. The society was patriarchal. The families were extended ones; that is, they had several generations living together. The oldest male member was the head of the family unit. So strong was this influence, that when a woman married, she was no longer considered her father's daughter, she joined her husband's family instead.

Customs in the Biblical Middle East changed very little through the centuries. So Paul's description of God's chain-of-command was probably observed in patriarchal times as well as in the New Testament church (see Ephesians 5:22,23): The woman was subject to the man, the man was subject to God. As the law applied to man, it in turn applied to woman.

But while the Old Testament extended the law only by logic, custom and implication, Paul, God's Christian lawyer, speaks clearly of female homosexuality in the New Testament.

In expounding on the historical guilt of mankind he says, "For the invisible things of him from the creation of the world are clearly seen, being understood by the things that are made, even his eternal power and Godhead; so that they are without excuse... Wherefore God also gave them up to uncleanness through the lusts of their own hearts, to dishonour their own bodies between themselves: who changed the truth of God into a lie, and worshipped and served the creature more than the Creator, who is blessed forever... For this cause God gave them up unto vile affections: for even their women did change the natural use into that which is against nature: and likewise also the men, leaving the natural use of the woman, burned in their lust one toward another; men with men working that which is unseemly, and receiving in themselves that recompence of their error which was meet" (Romans 1:20, 24-27).

The King James English perhaps clouds the reference, but there is little question that Paul refers to lesbian relationships in this passage. The words, "natural," "likewise" and the phrase "against nature" all demonstrate that the act of the women is the same sexual impurity as the act of the men. God has abandoned them to their sin. They will suffer the corruption of body and soul as their fitting penalty for their wrongdoing.

In both the Old Testament or Hebrew Bible and in the New Testament, the teaching is unmistakable. The Bible condemns the homosexual act for women as well as men. How, then, can intellectuals state that there is no reference to lesbianism anywhere in the Bible?

They are ignorant of the Word and the Spirit.

Now we can better understand the meaning of Peter's words, "But there were false prophets also among the people, even as there shall be false teachers among you, who privily shall bring in damnable heresies..." (II Peter 2:1).

They are teaching at this moment. They are using the Bible against itself. They are armed with a false doctrine. They are invading our schools and our churches. They write some of the television shows and motion pictures shown today. They engage us in their web of half-truths at work, in our clubs and service organizations. They seem sincere. They are scholars, and they themselves may not even be gay. They are like you and me. They are the Russells of the world. I would love to talk to Russell again, knowing what I know now.

Oh, how I wish I could go back to the Cottage.

8
Color the Church "Gay"

I was shaving on that early Good Friday morning and cut myself when I heard it. And it is hard to cut yourself with an electric razor, but then, what I heard was hard to take.

As is my habit, I had the small TV set in our bedroom tuned to one of the network morning news shows. It's my way of catching up on overnight world developments before breakfast. On this particular morning there had been the usual kinds of news—another hot spot or two in Africa, economic gloom and doom, details on the latest congressional investigations and, since it was the Friday before Easter, a story on the ways in which people around the globe were preparing to celebrate and observe the holy Sunday. And then toward the end of the newscast came the bombshell.

"A spokesman for the National Council of Churches," the commentator began to read in his faultless tones, "says 'it's simply not true' that the Bible has a 'single and clear position on homosexuality.' He says the Bible does not teach that it is 'a sin.'"

"Ouch!" I yelled. Blood trickling down my chin, I ran from the bathroom to the bedroom. But the commentator had given no further details and had turned the show back to the hosts in the network's New York studio who were giving the cue for the next commercial break.

At breakfast, nursing my sore chin, I searched the newspaper for more complete details. I finally found them way back on page forty under the headline, "Churchman hits anti-gay effort."

The newspaper version added little to the TV story, except that it gave the spokesman's name, Reverend G. William Sheek, director of the National Council's Family Ministries and Human Sexuality program, and said that he made his statements in response to Anita Bryant's Save Our Children campaign. He based his views on the work of a theologian at a

Chicago seminary.

For the next week, I watched both major newspapers in my hometown for some kind of rebuttal in the letters-to-the-editor column. None were printed.

It was just another in a series of events and reports which together remind me of a rainy-days-game my mother would play with me when I was four or five. It was a variation of the popular tot's finger game, "This Is the Church." All children used to learn that game at a tender age. I knew the finger-movements, but during inclement weather, my mother and I played it with a pencil and paper.

"This is the church," my mother would begin, drawing a square box on the paper, "and this is the steeple." A long, narrow triangle would be appended to the top of the box. My mother always drew her triangles a little lop-sided.

It really didn't bother me, because her heart was in the right place, and together we'd make up a long willy-nilly rhyme quite different from the traditional one that went with the finger actions. After all, our rhyme had to accommodate the drawing of windows, doors, people, trees and cars in the parking lot outside the church. Come to think of it, my mother was never very good at drawing cars either.

Once the drawing and the improvised rhyme were finished, I would take my crayons and color the picture while my mother went on about her housework.

In those days, we attended a church which had been built of native granite, so I'd carefully color the walls gray. To me, I guess, it just wasn't a church unless it had rock gray walls. My mother would study my completed artwork and almost always say, "That's nice, sweetheart, but I think a church is such a bright, sunny place to go. Next time, why don't you use a color for its outside that is more bright and gay?"

Well, the years of childhood and innocence are behind. We all play a much more adult game now. The church is being colored "gay" and not with crayons. And not, certainly, for the reason my mother had in mind. It is being colored by act and deed. . . .

A well-known minister announces his gayness to a surprised

81

congregation.

One of America's major Protestant denominations makes news not only by ordaining women to its priesthood, but by ordaining a woman who is an avowed lesbian. The bishop who is responsible for that ordination expresses his "amazement" at the "enormous amount of mail" the action prompts. But he refuses to withdraw his support of the lesbian because, "she is highly qualified by training and temperament to be a priest," and says the ordination is "not some sort of gesture condoning homosexuality or licentiousness." While many are outraged, the bishop cites others who support his action as "courageous and important."

The Catholic Church is said to have "over one-hundred" organizations for gays. Prominent among these is "Dignity." While Dignity does not "condone" homosexuality, its publicized aim is to help homosexuals to "stop agonizing, stop hating themselves and find peace of mind and freedom from guilt."

Church sponsored gay groups in mainline denominations hold dances and "singles" events for the gays in their communities. Some of these are promoted as being for "young homosexuals between the ages of thirteen and twenty," and some are attended by gays dressed as the opposite sex.

An evangelical church votes a homosexual male couple into membership. The pastor is pleased at the way the heterosexual congregation accepts the couple so freely. He claims the couple is discreet about their gayness. "I'm not sure that all of the congregation knows the full story," he says, "because while the 'boys' always come together in the same automobile, they never hold hands at church functions." He boasts that one of the homosexuals serves as the church treasurer and the other has been elected to the Board of Deacons.

The denomination of which this church is a member holds a national seminar on homosexuality for pastors and lay leaders. The purpose of the seminar seems to be to integrate homosexuals into the mainstreams of the church while minimizing "bigoted" opposition.

A transsexual applies for membership in the Baptist church

he attended as a man, explaining that he became "a woman" in response to Christ's command in Matthew 5:29, "And if thy right eye offend thee, pluck it out. . . ."

A report by the Quaker church concludes, "Homosexuality is no more deplorable than left-handedness."

The occurrences and the media coverage of them are proliferating at an incredible rate. Probably no other institution in our society has been caught up in the spreading homosexual controversy as has the Christian church.

"No other organization in modern times has suppressed homosexuality as much as the church," one writer states. "If the church accepts homosexuals as people, so will the rest of society."

A Christian commentator has said, "The church is the logical battleground when it comes to homosexuality. We are supposed to show concern for our fellow men. We are not supposed to judge. If we judge homosexuals too harshly, if we condemn them, if we take a legalistic approach, we will make ourselves the laughing stock of the world. To mishandle the problem of homosexuals in our midst will do more harm for the cause of Christ than it will do good. We are in the spotlight of public opinion and we had better not stub our collective toe."

What should the church do about homosexuality? How should it react to homosexuals?

Some churchmen view the gays with hostility. They deplore them as "the most contemptible creatures under the sun."

According to other sincere church folk, the vital thing is not gayness or un-gayness, but whether the homosexual is fulfilled as a person. They say God accepts individuals regardless of who or what they are. Man has been made acceptable to God by the sacrifice of Christ. Thus, if man has been made acceptable to God, he should be acceptable to all Christians, and that goes for the homosexual as well as the heterosexual.

In short, the church is caught in a dichotomy of principle which has the potential to shake it to its very foundations. On the one hand, we have the desire of the Christian to obey God's laws. On the other, we have the admonition to "love one another," the very core around which Christian practice is to be built. Did not Christ, Himself, give us this understanding when He answered the scribe who asked what was the "greatest commandment"? "And Jesus answered him, The first of all the commandments is, Hear O Israel; The Lord our God is one Lord: And thou shalt love the Lord thy God with all thy heart, and with all thy soul, and with all thy mind, and with all thy strength: this is the first commandment. And the second is like, namely this, Thou shalt love thy neighbour as thyself. There is no other commandment greater than these" (Mark 12:29-31).

This great philosophy has led one homophile scholar to draw the implication that Christianity has much in common with homosexuality. He says homosexuality has a great deal to do with passiveness and submission. As it is based on sexual inversion, he says, so Christian ideals are based on inversion of thought and circumstance: "But many that are last, shall be first" (Matthew 19:30); "Blessed are the meek: for they shall inherit the earth" (Matthew 5:5), a direct contradiction of the actuality of world order, in which the aggressive and the strong are in control: "...Love your enemies, do good to them that hate you, Bless them that curse you, and pray for them which despitefully use you. And unto him that smiteth thee on one cheek offer also the other; and him that taketh away thy cloak forbid not to take away thy coat also" (Luke 6:27-29).

"In a hundred ways . . . a person is told to go north in order to arrive south," the homophile states. "One central mechanism in all these examples (as in all inversions . . .) is clear: it is to dominate by submitting."

This pro-gay scholar is trying to make us believe that Christianity is—or should be—homosexual in aspect, saying, as homosexuality violates the "natural" order of things, Christianity does likewise. It is not "natural," he says, for men to love their enemies, to pray for those who would exploit them, to give to those who would steal their possessions. Thus, he reasons, the church should welcome homosexuals with open arms, because the two groups share "unnaturalness in common." In fact, the Christian church is the "much more dangerous" of the two, according to this fellow, because it uses "inversion to control men's minds," while homosexuality only "seeks to control men's bodies."

Now, most churches have not stretched the Golden Rule to such proportions—committing apostasy by misreading Christ's proclamation of love as a proclamation of "tolerance." And this, in turn, forces them to abandon or, at least, subordinate God's moral law as "too legalistic." They tend to forget or ignore the intolerance Christ displayed toward the Temple moneychangers (Matthew 21 and Mark 11), and toward the Pharisees and Sadducees of the New Testament era. Often, they don't even want to hear about it.

Using my theatrical training, I perform dramatic sermons in churches all over the country. My most popular work is titled, "They Who Knew Him." In it, I play six different characters who might have known Jesus during his thirty-three years in human flesh. One of the characters which I portray is one of the moneychangers who describes how Christ drove him and his colleagues from the Father's house. The scene is a kind of "documentary fiction," in that while based on the truth of the Scripture, the dialogue is an invention of mine.

When I first began performing "They Who Knew Him," I consulted with a number of pastors from different denominations to make certain that the work was theologically sound. One minister stopped me as I read him the moneychanger scene. "The line about Jesus being 'angry' will have to go," he said. "In my church we teach that Jesus was incapable of anger. He loved everyone. And most of all, He was tolerant."

This minister represents the breed of Christian modernists who deny God's punishment for sin. They just don't believe that our loving God could ever get angry, despite the fact that the Bible specifically mentions the "anger of the Lord" at least seventy-seven different times!

At the other end of the spectrum, there is another strain of Christians who overemphasize the wrath of God, rather than the love of God. They insist upon rigid adherence to their code of righteousness. They can name all of the Biblical sins plus a long list of sins which they have identified out of their own parochialism. They are narrow-minded to the point of pettiness. They claim that their interpretation is the correct one and that anyone who disagrees with them is in error. While they espouse the grace of God, theirs is actually a salvation of works. They are like the Pharisees who proudly wore parts of the Torah in little boxes tied to their foreheads and left arms to show men how pious and upright they were while their hearts were desolate (see Matthew 23).

Both the Tolerationists and the Intemperate Intolerationists are to me guilty of apostasy. Both groups put me in mind of the little book of Jude in the New Testament which says, "For there are certain men crept in unawares, who were before of old ordained to this condemnation, ungodly men, turning the grace of our God into lasciviousness, and denying the only Lord God, and our Lord Jesus Christ" (Jude 4).

Lasciviousness combines lustfulness and wantonness. It is easier to see how it can be fostered by the views of the Tolerationists than by the Intolerationists who preach their own strict brand of piousness. But, remember, it is *their* brand of piety as opposed to God's piety as taught in Scripture. To those sins identified by the Bible, they add many others until anything they don't like or don't understand or don't agree with has been branded a "transgression," with their views "sanctified" by an elaborate adaptation of God's Word.

You see, there is another aspect of "wantonness" that many in the church conveniently overlook in their zeal. In the dictionary sense, a wanton person is not necessarily an "immoral" person. A wanton person can sometimes be one who is a trifler in insignificance or one who indulges in excesses of conduct and language. By going beyond the code of morality prescribed by our Lord, they are guilty of wantonness, and hence, every bit as apostate as the Tolerationists.

The book of Jude continues, "Even as Sodom and Gomorrah, and the cities about them in like manner, giving themselves over to fornication, and going after strange flesh, are set forth for an example, suffering the vengeance of eternal fire. Likewise also these filthy dreamer defile the flesh, despise dominion, and speak evil of dignities" (Jude 7).

Isn't it interesting that Jude binds apostasy to the mark of

Sodom and Gomorrah? It teaches that apostasy and homosexuality go hand-in-hand.

The trouble with apostasy is that it makes tolerable what God has stamped intolerable and makes intolerable what God labels tolerable. The real danger of apostasy is it can appear so reasonable.

In my teens, I would hear the word "apostasy" and picture hard-hearted individuals deliberately turning their backs on God. I'd hear of "backsliders" and conjure up images of depraved persons participating in drunken orgies, their mouths fairly foaming with greed and lust.

But the mature view, I think, shows us that apostasy is much more subtle than that. The most treacherous apostates are often those who appear the most godly, the most reasonable. They might wear conservative clothing or dress in the fashion of the hour. Whichever the case, they will probably clutch a Bible under their arms. They teach the "truth of the Scriptures," but with a twist. They subvert the word and intention of God by preaching and professing the word and the intention colored by their own unidentified opinions.

The creeping apostasy in the church at all levels in all denominations poses a difficult dilemma for the born-again Christian and the Biblically bound congregation when it comes to homosexuality. Should the gays be brought into open fellowship in a church without apology, or is that an apostatic approach? Should the homosexual, then, be denied fellowship? Should he or she be cut off entirely, or is that an apostatic approach?

"It seems to me," Dr. Lynn Buzzard writes, "a biblical view [of homosexuality] rejects both of these alternatives. A biblical view must be informed by the two great traits of Scripture—truth and love. The hardest thing in the world is to combine those two."

Just how tough the synthesis of Scriptural truth and love can be is demonstrated by the variety of statements and stands being assumed in traditional Christian circles. For example, in Minneapolis in March of 1977, the American Lutheran Church issued a three page document which concluded that homosexuals "should be accepted for church membership." The Associated Press summary of the statement said it was the work of the ALC's Standing Committee on Research and Analysis and was designed to "stimulate thinking, promote discussion and motivate informed Christian response."

The paper called for "equality under the law" for gays and asked church congregations to "change their attitudes and actions toward homosexual persons."

However, the statement continued that "the message of the Scripture clearly is that homosexual behavior is a sin and contrary to the new life in Christ."

The committee noted that the church should not be involved in the arguments concerning the cause of homosexuality. They made it plain that they felt this was something to be determined by the various scientific disciplines, but they did ask that members of the American Lutheran Church extend to homosexuals the chance to take part in Christian worship and "to receive Christian ministry." They urged American Lutherans to "be more understanding of and more sensitive to life as experienced by the homosexual person."

Despite the statements of sympathy and support for gays, the committee wanted to make it clear that the recognition of the spiritual needs of homosexuals did not give sanction to gay behavior.

The ALC paper is representative of the manner in which Christians in the mid-nineteen seventies are striving to deal with the homosexual controversy. Over and over again we admit we know it is a "sin," but we are told it is a "sin" that needs "a special understanding." And over and over again, emphasis is placed upon the idea that the cause of homosexuality should have something to do with the attitude the church takes on the subject, but that the cause is unknown. The intimation seems to be drawn that, until science can supply the answers, the church should tentatively accept homosexuals, but on a guarded basis. If we wait long enough, they say, science can provide the solution and take the ultimate burden of policy making away from the church.

But the Gay Invasion is moving too fast for slow and

deliberate judgments. How much time do we need, anyway? We've already had several thousands of years and we can afford no more time to wait for science to give us a hand in the decision making department. The Invasion is upon the church now and it is not going to go away or disappear or abate of its own accord.

As Christians, our recourse should not be to science in the first place, but first to the Bible. Science can support Biblical thought, it can never replace it. And in the illumination of the Scripture, we can understand the homosexual "imbalance" to be primarily and foremost a spiritual imbalance. The same imbalance of spirit which is responsible for all sin. The same root cause behind gayness in the twentieth century was responsible for Adam's fall, for the prophet Balaam's self-destruction, for Solomon's woes, for Mary Magdalene's harlotry, for Ananias and Sapphira's greed and for every other sin ever committed or yet to be committed by mankind. In all of these instances there were extenuating circumstances; there were environmental precipitates which could be blamed. For Adam there was Eve's urging; for Balaam there was the promise of rich gain; for Solomon there was the lure of idolatrous women; for Mary Magdalene, the men who patronized her prostitution and the need to survive; for Ananias and Sapphira, the rationale of keeping back a small portion of the proceeds from the sale of their own property. Good reasons for sin from man's point of view, but not enough in the judgment of God. For the reasons are but symptoms of the root cause; rebellion against God.

His ways seem too narrow. His offering too simple. We want more. We want a smoother path. We want a more meandering road with a lot of turn-offs for side trips. We just do not care for self-denial. And, as the Bible says, "wickedness be sweet . . ." (Job 20:12). "It is as sport to a fool to do mischief . . ." (Proverbs 10:23).

Jesus told us who incites this rebellion: "Ye are of your father the devil, and lusts of your father ye will do. He was a murderer [literally and figuratively for not only does he slay men with sin, he kills the truth with his lies] from the beginning, and abode not in truth, because there is no truth in him. When he speaketh a lie, he speaketh of his own: for he is a liar, and the father of it" (John 8:44).

James tells us exactly how the sin mechanism works, "But every man is tempted, when he is drawn away of his own lust, and enticed. Then when lust hath conceived, it bringeth forth sin: and sin, when it is finished, bringeth forth death" (James 1:14-15).

So the church should deal with homosexuality exactly as it deals with every other sin. We do not need science to show us how to do that. Although I have no doubt that someday science will bring forth valuable information about homosexuality, to say that we are awaiting those findings before vigorously attacking the cause through Christian action is nothing but an abdication of responsibility.

It is the church's duty to preach the gospel to gays and through the Holy Spirit help them be convicted of their sin.

However, the average church today is not prepared to deal with homosexuals overtly in their midst. This has brought some to suggest organization of special missions to the gay society. And, indeed, there are some groups now in operation, several of which are staffed and run by former homosexuals. The missions are too new to have any real track record, but they do appear to be having some success.

Within the structure of the established church, homosexuals have frequently insisted upon a right of not being condemned for their sexual preference. To avoid the condemnation, churches exclusively for gays have been founded. One of the earliest, the Metropolitan Community Church, has become the "mother church" for America's first homosexual denomination. There are Metropolitan Community Churches in Los Angeles, Philadelphia, San Francisco, Denver and Chicago and other major U.S. cities.

The Metropolitan Community Church was founded less than ten years ago by an avowed homosexual, Troy Perry, who had been a minister in a fundamental, evangelistic denomination. When his homosexuality became known, he was defrocked, his ordination withdrawn. He moved to Los Angeles and set up his gay church, much to the embarrassment of his former church.

Some of the Metropolitan Community Churches are evangelistic and growth oriented. Aside from their practice of homosexuality, they are quite conservative in doctrine. They believe in the deity of Jesus Christ. They believe in and preach the resurrection. They claim salvation by faith. They practice the ordinances of baptism and communion.

But the one thing which the Metropolitan Community Churches do not do is to preach the sin of homosexuality. They do not recognize it as a sin. They hold to the belief that the Bible condemns promiscuity and marital infidelity rather than homosexuality per se.

To put this belief into action, the church encourages homosexual marriages, complete with all the trappings of a normal church wedding. Some three hundred of these marriages are said to have been performed in California alone. "Spouse" and "friend" are used in place of "husband" and wife," otherwise the ceremony is said to be remarkably close to other Protestant wedding ceremonies, and the vows identical except for the substitutions just noted.

Reverend Perry expresses a preference for long-term monogamous partnerships. Although his own love life has "not been that exclusive," he allows, "after all, God has a permissive will . . . I believe there can be loving experiences, even in one night stands."

It is hard to say whether Perry is representative of the clergy of the Metropolitan Community Churches. All are practicing homosexuals, it is said, and all the congregations are gay or are sympathetic to gays. One newspaper reporter who attended a service at one of the churches wrote of his surprise at learning that some of the "women" in the congregation, who were dressed as modestly as the women in attendance at any other church in the city on that Sunday morning, were really men. He also related observing more of what he called "laying on of hands" than he would expect to see at other evangelical church services.

In early 1977, the Metropolitan Community Church in Boston applied for membership in the Massachusetts Council of Churches. When the application was denied, the church's leaders said they would continue their efforts to gain admission.

The Boston church said it had been founded in 1973, is ecumenical in nature, and is but one "of a dozen" gay churches organized under the Metropolitan Community designation in the Northeastern portion of the country.

The minister for the church, Edward T. Hougen, was quoted as saying that his denomination had applied for Council of Churches membership in an effort to promote a more complete understanding between homosexual and heterosexual Christians.

The religious press which filed the report said of the campaign by the Boston gays that it "was likely to spark further debate in Protestant denominations over how to treat homosexuals. While most church leaders agree gays should not be ostracized, some still insist homosexuality is a sin—a view most gays consider outdated."

Outdated? Sometimes it does sadly seem so.

Psychologist Ralph Blair leads a New York organization called Evangelicals Concerned which holds that homosexuality is consistent with Biblical Christianity.

A homosexual was ordained by the United Church of Christ a few years back, and in 1976, the United Presbyterian Church announced it had a candidate for its ministry who was an avowed and practicing gay. But the UPC General Assembly countered by stating that it did not support homosexual ordinations or think them appropriate "at this time." The United Methodist Church has also given in to a conservative group in its ranks and has withdrawn efforts to induct homosexuals into its clergy, at least for the moment.

But the day is fast fading in the church when homosexuals are banished from the congregation. Church leaders are searching out gays in an effort to demonstrate the new liberality of religion. Some Christians find the shift shocking.

Jesus shocked some of the people in the religious organization of His day, too. He was a man ahead of His time. He scandalized the most important religious officials by socializing with publicans and sinners. When the scribes and Pharisees criticized Him for it, He replied to them, "They that are whole need not a physician; but they that are sick" (Luke 5:31).

What is the difference between what Jesus did and the way in which church modernists are associating with the gay cause? The answer is found in the very next verse. Continuing His thought, Jesus said, "I came not to call the righteous, but sinners to repentance" (Luke 5:32).

Jesus did not say, "It's OK to go on sinning. Do whatever you will, it's all right with Me." Jesus called for the publicans and sinners to repent. They were to feel sorrow and remorse over what they had done. They were to be contrite, not proud of their wrongdoing. Jesus' message was "Go and sin no more."

When He sent His disciples out two by two, ". . . they went out, and preached that men should repent" (Mark 6:12). After His resurrection He appeared to the twelve and gave them their commission, "Thus it is written, and thus it behoved Christ to suffer, and to rise from the dead the third day: And that repentance and remission of sins should be preached in his name among all nations, beginning at Jerusalem" (Luke 24:46, 47).

Peter at Pentecost said unto the multitude, "Repent, and be baptized every one of you in the name of Jesus Christ for the remission of sins, and ye shall receive the gift of the Holy Ghost" (Acts 2:38).

"Then they that gladly received his word were baptized: and the same day there were added unto them about three thousand souls. And they continued stedfastly in the apostles' doctrine and fellowship . . ." (Acts 2:41, 42).

No one can claim the grace of God, no one can enter into fellowship with God and the church without first repenting of his sins. It was this idea that became a moving force in the preaching and teaching of the first Christians.

Sinners were accepted into the congregation of Christ, but only after they had renounced their former lifestyles. We have evidence of this in I Corinthians 6:9-11. Remember, that's the passage in which Paul gives a list of those who will not inherit the kingdom of God. It included fornicators and homosexuals, among others. And then Paul said, "And such were some of you: but ye are washed, but ye are sanctified, but ye are justified in the name of the Lord Jesus, and by the Spirit of our God."

The operative tense is *were*. They had repented and put those things behind them. They had been born again in a new birth.

A longtime activist in the Gay Liberation Movement, Guy Charles, found Christ and it changed his life. He now conducts a ministry to homosexuals around the world. He says the Scriptures on homosexuality cannot be compromised. However, he says Christians cannot condemn the gay lifestyle without calling homosexuals "to repentance and healing in Christ."

A church Bible study group put it so well when they wrote an open letter to their bishop who had ordained a confessed lesbian to the Episcopal priesthood. They asked the bishop if she had "really repented" of her sin, or if she was still a practicing gay. "If so," they wrote, "this would seem a real impediment to her exercising her priesthood."

They noted that they were not called to judge the lesbian, but "we are called only to uphold a standard. That standard is that homosexuality is a sin, just as ordinary and forgivable as all other sins."

That seems to me to sum up the role the Christian church should be assuming in the struggle with the Gay Invasion. We can show Christian love and concern for gay people, but we cannot condone what they do. We must talk to them of repentance.

But, then, repentance is a good idea for all sinners is it not?

The church must build on the granite rock of the foundation of Jesus Christ. We must know where we're going and what has to be done, or they will color us "gay."

And what of our government and our educational institutions if the church surrenders its role?

Ouch!

9
If Rulers Hearken to Lies

They say she was the "first" acknowledged homosexual elected to public office. They say she will not be the last.

Her name is Elaine Noble. She used to have a talk show on the radio station run by Boston University. It was called, "The Gay Way." In 1973 and 1974, she served on the Massachusetts' Governor's Commission on the Status of Women. She has been twice elected to the Massachusetts state legislature, winning her seat by campaigning for the rights of the elderly, the poor and the homosexual. Her committee assignments have included Education and Ethics. On the latter committee, she has worked to draw up a code of conduct for Massachusetts' house members.

To think it was not so many years past that more than one politician rode to victory at the polls on a campaign of moral reform. A district attorney could become mayor of his city, or even governor of his state by cracking down on vice. Sweeping raids were often conducted against known gay establishments. An opponent could be easily defeated by sensational charges of homosexuality lodged against him, whether the charges were true or false. At least one United States senator was able to win a national reputation by conducting wide scale investigations of Communist and homosexual activity within the government.

Of course, homosexuality is not the only kind of sexual activity to give rise to political scandal and titillating headlines. A number of U.S. senators and congressmen have had their careers ruined when reports of their heterosexual misdeeds were made public.

Sex in politics has always been and always will be big news. It was and is a highly emotional issue certain to bring public comment, critical outcries and to swing votes. But never in American history has so-called "illicit sex" been more asset than liability as it is currently.

And it surely was not an asset in Judah of 700 B.C. At least, not to godly men and women. We have the record of Isaiah to show us that. Isaiah, you see, was a politician and statesman as well as a mighty prophet of the Lord God, Yahweh. There is some evidence to suggest he was the leader of one of three political parties abroad in Jerusalem in those days.

He spoke often of the corruption and greed in government. In one fiery oration filled with prophecy and political observations, he spoke specifically of the homosexual influence in Judean rule. He said, "The shew of their countenance doth witness against them: and they declare their sin as Sodom, they hide it not. Woe unto their soul: for they have rewarded evil unto themselves . . . .

"As for my people, children are their oppressors, and women rule over them. O my people, they which lead thee cause thee to err, and destroy the way of thy paths" (Isaiah 3:9 and 12).

In the last verse, the word "women" has sometimes been rendered "women-like or effeminate men." Other sources say that the passage refers to "manlike women," women who have assumed the role of leadership traditionally reserved for men. Whichever it is, Isaiah was definitely speaking out against the "unnatural" presence in government.

If Isaiah's speech had been covered by the American press of our age, the report might read something like this:

"CONSERVATIVE LEADER CONDEMNS WOMEN AND GAYS IN GOVERNMENT"

Jerusalem (JP)—At a rally held today on the Temple steps here, Isaiah Bar Amoz, Chairman of the right-wing God Party expressed extreme displeasure over the growing role of women and homosexuals in government.

"These people flaunt their 'unnatural tendencies,' " Isaiah told the audience. "Their childish and selfish aims are leading this country toward destruction."

Isaiah called upon the nation to "swing from the politics of the new-left and take up the old fashioned values of their grandparents."

While many in the large crowd estimated at over 3,000 cheered, they were mostly those people over forty. The younger members of the audience were swift in giving their reactions.

One young woman who said she was a spokesperson for the Women's Equality organization (WE), called Isaiah's speech, "A typical male chauvinist scare tactic designed to keep women in a subservient stereotype role and thus deprive them of their rights as persons."

Another man carrying an "I'm Gay and Proud" placard agreed, stating, "He's a part of the establishment who would deny all minorities their right to be heard, their right to hold a decent job and their right to participate in government. His presence offends me. He cares more about his religion than he does the feelings of people."

Isaiah Bar Amoz, long known for his unorthodox conservatism, spoke for approximately forty-five minutes. His speech was interrupted several times by catcalls and boos. At one point, his supporters and detractors engaged in a shouting match which threatened a riot, until the demonstrators withdrew from the scene.

Naturally, this news story is fictional to the extent that, as far as we know, there were no newspapers in the eighth century before Christ; and in that the Bible, by and large, does not report the reactions of the people to whom Isaiah spoke. But the point is, Judah was far more like America today than any of us would probably care to imagine.

Politicians in that day, as in ours, issued advanced copies of their prepared remarks for dissemination to their followers. This is the way some of the Bible was preserved. And gayness was much in fashion, imported from such countries as Assyria, Babylon and Egypt. People probably did make political placards. In fact, we have the recorded incident of Isaiah, himself, writing a message on a large scroll for purposes of holy propaganda.

And, while he did criticize the women, he did not necessarily do it because he felt them to be inferior to men. He did it because they were "haughty" (Isaiah 3:16). That is, they were insolent and more proud than they had a right to be.

Today, many would have us believe the Bible is anti-woman. That it teaches the woman's "only place" is in the home. That simply is not the case. The Bible teaches the worth of a woman. It teaches she has a place in service to her church and her Lord. It also teaches that she can be a leader of people when she is properly prepared, when the time is right in God's plan. Read the story of Deborah, the woman who judged Israel, in the book of Judges starting with the fourth chapter, and you will find the Scripture is far from chauvinistic. It preaches the true liberation of women in God and Christ.

Isaiah saw the high and mighty attitude of the women in Judah and the homosexuality of its men for what they were: symptoms of the drive for selfish gratification. The Pleasure Syndrome. It took a hundred and fifty years, but it finally did destroy the nation as Isaiah had predicted.

The Pleasure Syndrome destroyed the powerful Grecian and Roman civilizations, too. Both of these cultures are often held forth as examples of societies in which homosexuality flourished and thereby prospered the living standards of their peoples. There is no doubt that lovely specimens of art, literature, architecture and science have survived from the times at which homosexuality was at its zenith in Greece and Rome. But we must not forget that wide-spread homosexual practice immediately preceded the fall of both nations.

Again, it was not homosexuality in and of itself which caused the downfall of these great powers. It was but a symptom of the real cause: the selfish lust for pleasure.

Our search for pleasure is growing as well. And not only in the secular life, but also in the church. We build huge edifices in which to worship. Sometimes they border on the ostentatious. We try to make our sojourns in the houses of our living God as comfortable and as pleasurable as money and resource will allow.

The drive for self-gratification takes many forms, not the

least of which is homosexuality. And homosexuality has certainly made itself felt in American political circles. The U.S. government has in fact had more than its share of gays in its service during its history.

One of the most celebrated homosexuals to serve in government prior to the twentieth century was Walt Whitman, poet and male nurse, who served as a clerk in the War Department during the Lincoln years.

Also during the War Between the States, a female transvestite, Dr. Mary Walker, was appointed an assistant surgeon in the Union army. She was captured by the Confederates and imprisoned. In 1865, she was given the Medal of Honor for meritorious service to her country. A federal review board withdrew the honor as "undeserved" in 1917. It is doubtful she was a lesbian and she did publish several reasonably moral books on the subject of sex. But she is an example of the sexual variation our government has tolerated from time to time.

In more modern times, "every President from Franklin Roosevelt forward has had homosexuals in his administration," says a political historian.

Roosevelt, it is known, had to personally intercede to keep one of his highly placed diplomatic appointees from being the center of a homosexual scandal. The man was a presidential courier during World War II and subsequently held a variety of other important posts, including that of acting head of the Department of State. He was so overtly gay, he kept his staff as well as the President of the United States hopping to keep his name out of the newspapers and to keep civil complaints against him hushed.

A congressman who served several terms on Capitol Hill was said to "make no effort to hide his sexual preference," while in the nation's capital, but managed to carefully mask his homosexuality from his constituents back home.

"In fact, homosexuality has occasionally been so easily accepted at the upper echelons of government that not just quiet private lives but overt misbehavior has sometimes been tolerated against staggering odds," a researcher in the field of homosexuality revealed.

The same man also noted homosexuals are commonly sought out for their particular tendencies and employed in government. Others are employed with complete ignorance of their sexual proclivity.

The most extensive anti-gay campaign in our nation's history was carried out by Congress in the late nineteen forties and early fifties. The investigations have variously been branded "witch hunts," "hypocritical shams," and "sincere attempts to return government to morality." Just which description is the most accurate remains for future generations to judge.

Senator Joseph McCarthy gave the era its popular name, since he was the leading protagonist. But there were many other senators involved, some preceding McCarthy.

Some have said, McCarthy himself was latently homosexual. The theory is, the strong anti-homosexual is trying to protect himself from public detection and self-revelation.

But as we have seen, this is often a technique of smear and doubt used against those who would fight homosexuality and is as much a deceit as the unfounded charge of "gay" when offered without proof. In McCarthy's case, the evidence is unclear as to whether he was or was not. The man is dead and unable to give his side of the story.

However, in the late forties and early fifties, he was very much alive and very active in the campaign against communists and homosexuals in government. To understand the implications of the McCarthy investigations, we must understand something of the national situation of that day.

The post-World War II period had seen the rapid rise of the Union of Soviet Socialist Republics as a major world power. The atomic bomb which closed the war in the Pacific had inaugurated a new and frightening potential for instantaneous world destruction. It was a very scary prospect in very jittery times. Coupled with a growing technology and increased animosity in Soviet-American relations, there was a logical concern for internal security.

FBI agents had uncovered an American Communist Party with "cells" throughout the country who were bent upon the overthrow of the United States government. The Communist

.threat was real enough, or so it seemed in 1947.

Homosexuals were included in the investigations as "security risks," because it was thought they were more subject to blackmail than their heterosexual counterparts and—expert witnesses of that day agreed—less stable in personality.

Perhaps there were those who recalled the way in which the Germans had tried to reach homosexuals in sensitive positions during the war. Only five years before the McCarthy era investigations began, Naval Intelligence and the Federal Bureau of Investigation had uncovered a Brooklyn house of male prostitution. Some of its visitors and residents were known Nazi agents. The purpose was to gather information about U.S. shipping of vital war supplies to the European theatre of conflict.

Most alarming was the fact that one of the regular American visitors to the place was a prominent member of the congressional delegation from Massachusetts who also happened to be the chairman of Naval Affairs. He was apparently so valuable to the U.S. conduct of the war, that orders went out from the highest quarters of government to quash the part of the investigation involving him.

But insiders in Washington knew the full story and it was undoubtedly fresh in their minds when the first tentative steps were taken to purge the government of "subversives" and "perverts" in the late forties.

It is true that much of the charges and counter-charges were based on hearsay and innuendo, but there was quite a bit of hard evidence presented, too; much more than contemporary apologists would lead you to believe. The head of the Washington D.C. police vice squad estimated there were five thousand homosexuals in the nation's capital at that time, with thirty-seven hundred in government service. His figures were considered highly suspect by a few newspapermen who thought them greatly inflated, and claimed the police department had a list of only two hundred known gays. Other observers felt the estimate of three thousand plus gays in government was too conservative.

Between 1947 and April of 1953, four hundred and twenty-five employees were dismissed from the State Department for homosexual inclinations. In 1955, it was reported that during the first sixteen months of the Eisenhower administration another six hundred and fifty-five more persons were either "suspected" or dismissed for sexual deviations.

It is a sad possibility that a percentage of the more than one thousand government workers who came under suspicion or were fired during the McCarthy era were judged guilty on faulty evidence, hearsay gossip and association. A number may have been innocent. But there is a great movement abroad in our land presently, which would have us believe that *all* were innocent. And it just is not so. After a careful and thorough reading of the available records, it is my considered opinion that the majority got exactly what they deserved in spite of—and not because of—Senator McCarthy's tactics.

Frankly, McCarthy was not my kind of politician. From what I've read of his life and style, I think he was an opportunistic, publicity-seeking coveter of votes. He played on the emotionalism of his constituency. His modus operandi bordered on the savage and was both unethical and patronizing. It was the man and his personality which were wrong, though, and not the cause. To say it tritely, we shouldn't throw out the baby with the bath water.

The legacy of the McCarthy era is neither all good nor all bad. On the plus side it demonstrated that we as a nation were vulnerable to invasion from within; it showed America could be guilty of excesses in many parts and, it revealed that "purges" seldom accomplish anything lastingly constructive. It is not more and better laws we need, not more investigations of investigations, but better people all around. In that light, we can see it is the church which will improve society, not the government.

The minuses of the McCarthy legacy include the destroyed lives of those who were innocent but convicted by gossip, the rift between the conservatives and the moderates over the ruthless abuse of power by a few of the zealots in the McCarthy camp, and the fostering of the gay rights movement.

There had been efforts before in the United States to establish an organized defense of homosexuals. However, none enjoyed the success of the Mattachine Society founded in the two years between 1948 and 1950 by an admitted Communist Marxist and avowed homosexual, Henry Hay. Hay's group was ostensibly established as "a service and welfare organization devoted to the protection and improvement of Society's Androgynous Minority." Its real reason for being was to battle "encroaching American Fascism" against gays. Anyway, that's what they called the investigations then being conducted by the House UnAmerican Activities Committee and Senator McCarthy.

The Mattachine Society was also referred to by the innocuous name of "Bachelors Anonymous," short for "International Bachelors Fraternal Order for Peace and Social Dignity." It made it sound like some kind of Friday night supper club which gathered to have a little fun by "girl watching." Nothing could have been farther from the reality.

Hay was a card carrying member of the Communist Party for eighteen years. In his own words, he was "a well-sought-after" teacher of Marxist principles for the Communists and for the Labor University of California. The original Mattachine Society was conceived as an underground group with a secret membership, much like the Communist party in America in the nineteen thirties.

Almost from the beginning, its literature contained phrases which have since become familiar catchwords, i.e., "police brutality," "a violation of our civil rights," and "minorities like homosexuals."

When he became so deeply involved in the gay movement, Hay went to the Communist Party and asked to be expelled from membership for the good of their cause. The communists refused his request, choosing instead to drop him from the membership rolls as "a security risk, but a lifelong friend of the people." This was done in honor of his eighteen years of Party membership.

The Mattachine Society remained a secret organization until the spotlight of national publicity was turned upon it by a rather seedy gossip magazine. It was one of the few good things the magazine did in its rather undistinguished and salacious life span. A year later, Hay was called to testify before the House UnAmerican Activities Committee.

His testimony was relatively brief. He denied having been a member of the Communist Party, although he had previously admitted it on many occasions. Through a mixup and in the confusion of the hearing room, the transcript of his potentially perjurious answer could not be found at that moment, so he was never charged. To the rest of the Committee's questions, he pled the Fifth Amendment.

About the time Hay was making his command appearance before the HUAC, a group of lesbians busied themselves in the organization of a secret society for female homosexuals. They dubbed it the "Daughters of Bilitis," a name chosen because it had deep gay significance, but sounded as if it was a poetry reading society or a group similar to the "Daughters of the American Revolution." As the movement grew, the DOBs changed the flavor of their group from one of secrecy to one openly declared in purpose and intent. The State of California and the Federal government both recognized it as "a legitimate nonprofit corporation" in 1957, bestowing upon it tax-exempt status.

There were other homosexual groups, but the Mattachine Society and the Daughters of Bilitis plus an organization called "One" comprised the nucleus of the burgeoning gay aggregation. They began to hold national conventions in major cities around the country, each more widely publicized and open than the one before. They campaigned in behalf of candidates sympathetic to the gay cause. They lobbied against anti-gay laws at the state and local level and for pro-homosexual legislation. They sought and received interviews on radio and television programs in such cities as New York, Los Angeles, San Francisco and Denver. And, they began to seek the aid of major Christian denominations.

By January 1, 1965, they felt secure enough in their efforts to invite fifteen representatives of the clergy and their wives to a New Year's Gay Ball in San Francisco. The purpose was to raise funds for a newly formed "Council on Religion and the Homosexual." The men of the cloth and their spouses stood in a receiving line, welcoming over five hundred homosexuals to the affair.

Also in attendance were the uninvited guests—fifty members of the San Francisco Police Department who photographed arriving and departing participants at the ball and infiltrated the hall. The ministers present were furious. Along with their homosexual associates, they charged "police harassment of a minority and infringement of civil rights."

Four people were arrested and charged with interfering with the police. Defended by the American Civil Liberties Union, the four were freed with a directed verdict of "not guilty." Dissatisfied with the outcome, the four promptly sued the City of San Francisco for $1,500,000, because their trial had left unresolved the "issue of their civil rights."

But the fact remains, to the homosexual community, the 1965 New Year's Ball is an important date. "Its impact upon the religious community, on the police and the political scene, contributed indelibly," they say to the gay cause, because "the conspiracy of silence had been broken."

Another important date marked by gays everywhere and billed as "probably the biggest shot in the arm for the new [homosexual] aggression," by two lesbian spokespeople, was the end of Gay Pride Week in 1970, celebrated by Homosexual Liberation Day. Twenty thousand gays marched in New York and more in Los Angeles. They carried banners and wore T-shirts emblazoned with defiant slogans of Gay Pride. Chants of "Two-Four-Six-Eight, gay is just as good as straight!" "Gay is good!" and "Say it loud, gay and proud!" punctuated the bizarre parade. It was a staged media event which a sympathizer called, "a joyful, folksy, funky happy street" demonstration. It set the homosexual thrust for "a drive to freedom which will not be denied."

Proverbs 14:9 applies well to the scene when it says, "Fools make a mock at sin. . ." And Galatians 6:7 adds, "Be not deceived; God is not mocked: for whatsoever a man [and a nation] soweth, that shall he also reap."

Yet, the parades and demonstrations, the outcries against

discrimination aimed at homosexuals, the demand for gay civil rights, the strengthening of the new Gay Coalition and the Gay Liberation Front began to have their effect in the American political arena. Several states moved to liberalize their laws on sodomy and homosexual practices of "consenting adults." And the courts of the land began to strike down anti-homosexual ordinances. Gays began to take an active part in political parties. One of the floor whips at the 1976 Democratic Convention was an admitted practicing homosexual. And James Earl Carter, the Democratic candidate for the office of President of the United States began to boldly court the homosexual vote.

If elected, he promised, he would move immediately to federally decriminalize sodomy and related sexual acts. His stand was advertised to the homosexual constituency in full page advertisements appearing in gay publications. One such ad showed the candidate's wife, Rosalyn, engaged in conversation with two well-known gay leaders, Troy Perry of the Metropolitan Community Church and Dr. Newton Deiter. Gays worked actively in the Carter campaign and endorsed him time and again.

The candidate, who claimed to be a "born-again Christian," displayed rather radical views. He, himself, may have been well-intentioned, but to an observer removed from the action it almost seemed as if some backroom political strategist had said, "The elections these days are usually very close. A few votes can make the difference. The twenty million gays in America represent a lot of votes. Let's get 'em on our side."

In spite of predicted difficulty expected for Carter by leading evangelicals because of his homosexual stand, he was elected in a race distinguished by a close popular vote. And he began to move to make good on his campaign promises.

Only two months to the day after he was inaugurated, one of President Carter's aides, Margaret Costanza held a meeting in the White House with ten members of the National Gay Task Force.

The President and his family were away from the White House at the time of the three-hour session, but those taking part were assured the President was "aware of the meeting," according to newspaper accounts of March 27, 1977.

Jean O'Leary, the National Gay Task Force codirector told reporters, "This is the first time in the history of this country that a president has seen fit to acknowledge the rights and needs of some twenty million Americans."

She said, "We had a fantastic meeting. We got a commitment on all the issues we brought up."

Presidential aide Costanza made a promise to the participants that they would have the opportunity to take grievances to federal agencies and that her office would lend its power as a "door opener."

The gay grievances included two issues on which they demanded quick action. One was to upgrade less-than-honorable military discharges given for homosexual practices and the other was to stop discrimination by immigration officials against gays who wanted to enter the United States.

The group also lobbied for research grants and more social services for homosexuals, better protection of homosexual prisoners, an extension of tax deductible status to more gay organizations, and the lifting of bans against homosexuals serving in the military which also deprived gays of veterans benefits.

The White House meeting was described by a Task Force member as "a happy milestone on the road to full equality under the law for gay men and women." The gays said the discussion demonstrated the President's commitment "to human rights."

Outside a small story relating Anita Bryant's criticism of the White House meeting, opposition to the event slipped by largely unnoticed. Anita Bryant, though, said, "I protest the action of the White House staff in dignifying these activists for special privilege with a serious discussion of their alleged 'human rights.' "

"Alleged human rights" is right.

There are many other "minorities" denied the rights homosexuals claim they are denied. I volunteered for a hitch in the United States Army. I was promised an officer's commission.

107

But I happen to belong to that minority of degenerative arthritics. I was turned down because the Army didn't want to take a chance of paying me permanent disability for the rest of my life. The American taxpayer was spared, but what about my rights? The action denied me the right to earn veterans benefits.

Incidentally, this took place when the draft was still in force. I was classed as "1-Y" in the draft classification, the same category to which practicing homosexuals were also assigned.

Certainly, our Constitution guarantees each individual certain rights. Its Preamble states, "We the people of the United States, in order to form a more perfect union, establish justice, insure domestic tranquillity, provide for the *common* defense, promote the *general* welfare, and secure the blessings of liberty to ourselves and our posterity, do ordain and establish this Constitution for the United States of America."

"Perfect Union...." "Common defense...." "General welfare...." It doesn't take a Constitutional lawyer to understand that we are a nation ruled by the majority. Our laws· were once made for the good of that majority. In the majority is our liberty. And the majority is made up of many minorities. But each minority must compromise its rights for the rights of the common good. Liberty is not "license" to do anything, everything we please, to follow our own codes of conduct. We must follow the code set down by the state and by our God. That is what liberty really means.

David of Bethlehem knew this when in his great prayer hymn he sang, "So shall I keep thy law continually for ever and ever. And I will walk at liberty: for I seek thy precepts" (Psalms 119:44,45).

God's plan of redemption and rules thereof have set us free from sin. Without redemption there is no real freedom. The right of salvation is the only true "human right." Salvation is liberty.

The homosexual has the freedom to sin, the freedom to follow after his own lusts. But he does not have the right to flaunt it openly in front of me and my children. As he should be protected under the law, so should I. And I'm not singling homosexuals out, either. I do not believe promiscuous and permissive heterosexuals have the right to flaunt their conquests. I should have the right not to tolerate what I find abhorrent. Yes, liberty is not license.

The issue is not tolerance—anyway, not anymore. A spokesman for the Gay Libbers has openly stated in print, "Homosexuals today are not seeking tolerance; they are demanding total acceptance... No more polite discussions, no more secret societies, no more concern about the 'image.' Gay is Good! Once the bottle containing the genie is open, it is not easy to get the genie back into the bottle. The homosexual is out of the bottle—you will not get her/him back in!"

Who's trying to put them back in? Certainly not our government. Their political influence is far too strong.

On April 15, 1977, it was announced that Elaine Noble, the gay state representative from Massachusetts, was being considered for a high post in ACTION, the federal volunteer corps. It was rumored that she was being viewed for the post of domestic operations director, one of the top policy-making positions in the agency; a position which requires senate confirmation.

When the assistant to the director of ACTION was asked if he thought her homosexuality would be an issue in the confirmation hearings, he replied, "It's against the law in the District of Columbia to discriminate against homosexuals and we're bound to uphold the law."

I can appreciate Miss Noble's potential. Her talents appear considerable. But I cannot support the lie that homosexuality is acceptable in high places. Our leaders have accepted it, it appears. They hearken to it.

"If a ruler hearken to lies, all his servants are wicked," says Proverbs 29:12. That's the Biblical word on the subject. Think about it.

They say Miss Noble is the "first acknowledged homosexual considered for so high a government office. They say she will not be the last."

10
Suffer the Little Children

The world is full of them, stage mothers.

In popular literature they are portrayed as mean, witchy women who ruthlessly force their children into show business. By so doing, they are supposed to be realizing some thwarted ambition of their own which they are able to gain only vicariously through their offspring. They are the bane of directors and adult actors, the terror of casting people and agents, the courters of talent scouts and the smotherers of their sons and daughters.

The late Rosalind Russell played the archtype of the character in the motion picture "Gypsy." She was the mother who dragged her adolescent daughters from one sleezy vaudeville theatre to another in a hand-to-mouth existence, lying, stealing and panhandling, trying to get them their "big break." She finally compelled her girl, Gypsy, to become a strip tease "artist." The movie, and the stage musical it was adapted from, were based on the true story of Gypsy Rose Lee.

I encountered a few of these creatures both male and female, for there are stage fathers, too, in my theatrical career. They are every bit as bad, if not worse, than the fictional stereotype would lead you to believe. They drag little Johnnie or little Mary from dancing lessons to singing lessons to elocution lessons to acting lessons to piano and guitar lessons to auditions ad nauseam. They throw temper tantrums of gargantuan magnitude when a director fails to cast their "talented" child, and at the same time chastise the child unmercifully for his or her failure.

The first stage parents I ever met were the father and mother of a boy cast in the leading role of a children's stage production at the local civic theatre. The show was the classic, "Huckleberry Finn," and the boy, Andy, played Huck. Andy was eleven then and vitally interested in baseball. His fondest dream was to play first base in the Little League, but his parents wouldn't hear of it.

Andy's mother was in her late forties. Andy had been a "late baby," born long after the doctors had told his parents that they would never have children. They doted on him, or I should say, his mother doted on him and his father doted on her. She had been an aspiring actress in her girlhood but never made it beyond appearing in the senior class play in high school. She married when she was eighteen.

In those days, it was unseemly for a woman to pursue a career after marriage, unless she was widowed or her husband was seriously ill and unable to support her. So she settled into "a dreary life of housework and afternoon bridge clubs."

That's the way she described it to several cast members as we sat in the Green Room one Saturday afternoon between matinees. The "Green Room" in a theatre is usually adjacent to the stage. It is the place where actors can meet members of the audience after a show or relax in makeup between shows. When Andy was born, he became her ticket out of a lifestyle she could not bear and into the glamorous world of "show biz." She was bound and determined he was going to be the "male Shirley Temple." She gave him permanents because she believed curly-headed little boys had a better chance for stardom than boys with straight hair. She saw that he was always dressed in a suit with shirt and tie and made him wear a miniature snap-brimmed fedora hat whenever he went out. The only time the rest of us ever saw Andy in anything approximating the normal dress for boys was when he was in costume for his part as Huck.

Andy's father was worse. He wouldn't even let Andy play with the other children in the cast on rehearsal breaks, because he was afraid Andy would catch something from them like a cold or chicken pox which would keep him from performing. And this wasn't a professional production. It was an amateur show.

After "Huckleberry Finn" closed, Andy's dad quit his job and moved the family to Hollywood where they were sure Andy would "be discovered." The truth was, Andy was a terrible actor. He was stilted and totally uninspired. He would have been a much better baseball player. He would have had to be a much better baseball player, even if he couldn't hit or catch the ball, that's how bad he was on stage.

As far as I know, Andy never appeared in a movie or on television. Once, after I moved to Southern California, I tried to look the family up, but they weren't listed in the telephone book and I don't know what happened to him. He would be in his late twenties or early thirties now. I hope he became the baseball player he always wanted to be, but I doubt it. What chance did he have? More likely, he grew up to be a "crazy, mixed-up kid."

But most of the stage parents I knew after Andy's were not like his at all. They were the exception rather than the rule. Most stage mothers and fathers are permissive rather than ambitious. Their child has usually developed an interest in theatre on his own, and not wanting to deny the child anything, they let him participate to his heart's content.

I've seen such parents let their children stay out all hours of the night for rehearsals. I've seen them let their children attend after-the-show cast parties which certainly weren't fit for children, let alone most adults. I've seen such parents let their children take up with adults of questionable character because "it's good for them. They are interested and we don't want to do anything to inhibit or squelch their 'creative growth.' "

Of course there are stage parents who make every effort to see their children lead a "normal" life offstage. They encourage other interests and attempt to teach their offspring how to cope with the "real world."

I thank the Lord that my parents were not stage parents in any way, shape or form. They were supportive of my work in school plays, but would not let me appear in civic or professional drama until I was older. Even then, they often drove me to rehearsals and picked me up afterward. And, as long as I was living at home, I had to keep them informed as to where I was and who I was with and under no circumstance would they let me attend a cast party.

They made me go to Sunday School and church where I learned my dramatic talents could be used for the Lord, and they were quick to point out alternate professions which might interest me. During college, they insisted that in addition to my theatre major, I take a minor in a field which would prepare me for another means of making a living besides acting.

They saw every play I was in, and were proud of some of my theatrical achievements. But I am sure they breathed a collective sigh of relief when I married a Nebraska farm girl and forsook acting for family, church work and business.

I do not mean to make them sound like rigid disciplinarians for with them it was never discipline for discipline's sake. They spanked me and grounded me when I needed it, but they always tempered their actions with the best discipline of all, Christian love and understanding.

My folks were never caught up in the "permissiveness" which today characterizes so many stage parents as well as parents in general.

Unbridled permissiveness is everywhere it seems. Parents do not want to be guilty of "making" their children do anything. We have been brainwashed by educational modernists and self-proclaimed child rearing experts who for more than three decades have exerted the theory that discipline "warps" rather than guides.

One national newspaper related the story of a mother who found out her boy was gay. It happened on a Sunday morning, she said, while she was out shoveling the snow from the walks. She was cleaning the walks, because she felt it was easier than getting her son out of bed to attend to the chore. While she was thus engaged, the boy came to the door and asked her to "come in"; he needed to tell her something. The something was that he was homosexual.

The mother said she was "sick for weeks," wondering why the thing had happened to her son. I wonder if permissiveness had anything to do with it?

My own son is ten years old as I write this. Only last week he came to me and said, "Dad, I've got a girl friend."

"That's nice," I said. Kids frequently emulate the actions of older kids. I had not begun to really notice girls until I was in my early teens, but I realize children mature a little more quickly in the seventies. I was about to put his remark down to a child-hood crush when he continued, "Can I take her to a movie Friday night?"

"What?" I stammered.

"I want to ask her for a date."

"You're too young," I said, regaining myself. "You're only ten."

"Aw, Dad," he said, "I'm not too young. Other kids my age have lots of dates."

I thought he was exaggerating. But when I checked with some of the parents of children in his class at school, I found they were indeed allowing their ten-year-old sons and daughters to date. "If I don't, my boy might grow up to be a homo-sexual," one father told me with a straight face. His face was straight because he meant it.

Well, my son is not going to date until he is much older. His friends keep telling him he is "missing out," but if I let him date, he would be missing out on childhood. And, I have no fear my stand will make him grow up gay.

To say that denial of heterosexual dating privileges at ten is the cause of homosexuality at twenty, is a demonstration of ignorance, the kind of ignorance that plays directly into the hands of those "pushing" homosexuality upon our society.

Young people in their teens and twenties are eager for new experiences. They are constantly looking for something exciting. My fear is, if normal dating has been allowed from a very early age, in the restlessness of adolescence, children will look else-where to satisfy their need for adventure. The elsewhere might well be homosexuality for reasons which shall become clear presently.

We are a permissive and tolerant generation of parents. I am not certain whether permissiveness leads to tolerance or tol-erance to permissiveness. But we have both in massive quan-tities and it is our children who suffer.

A few years back, the big news was the epidemic of unwanted pregnancies and venereal disease which was sweeping through the teenage population. Premarital sex, it seemed, had become the national teen fad.

But instead of a public outcry over the morality of the situation, there was public pressure to help children by teaching them better means of birth and disease control; for treatment of VD without parental permission; for abortions for minors, again without parental knowledge or consent—and all aided and abetted by courts and educators.

The blame lay, the experts said, with the parents. Parents just were not teaching their children the facts of life early enough. They didn't, it was claimed, because they were constrained by an old-fashioned and false sense of morals. The children who were much more "hip" than the oldsters and much more freethinking, thanks to the enlightened culture in which they lived, were experimenting with sex without proper knowledge. Thus, because the parents were abdicating their responsibility, the educators said, they would step into the breech.

Sex education courses became mandatory in many public school systems across the land. And sex education for very young students, I might add.

One morning as our family sat around the breakfast table, our son, then six years old, casually and calmly explained all the Facts of Life to us, and I mean *all*. He had learned them from the eleven-year-old girl who lived across the street. And she had learned them from a mandatory sex class in her elementary school!

My wife and I found ourselves having a discussion of the sex morals taught in the Bible with our son far earlier than we would have ever dreamed. We had tried to protect our son from such knowledge, but the school system had denied our parental right. They did not do it directly, but they supplied information to a little girl who was too young to know how to handle it.

And the same people who gave us sex education, now want to give us homosexual education.

They want to do it by putting acknowledged homosexual teachers in public schools. When we protest, they smugly say, they're already there, "you just don't know it." To substantiate their statement, they offer the explanation that the teaching profession "has always had a high percentage of homosexuals in its ranks."

Pressed for the actual statistics, they will say, "anywhere between fifty and eighty-five percent," and then add, "in some schools."

It is the same old story. We are supposed to give gays acceptance in any given field because they are already in the field in a large quantity. Such general statistics are hard to contradict because they are hard to get in the first place. They are hard to obtain for the very reason given as to why we are not aware of the homosexuals already involved. These "poor" individuals cannot declare themselves, we are told, because if they did, they would lose their jobs.

If they are already in the classroom, then what is the controversy about? They want to stop hiding their homosexuality and come out in the open without fear of reprisal. They want to declare their gayness to your child and mine.

They deny they would use their teaching positions to "recruit" youngsters into their lifestyle as Anita Bryant and others fear. All they desire, the gays say, is to provide "positive role-models" so heterosexual children can see homosexuals are not "terrible monsters" to be frightened of, but just ordinary citizens who happen to like their sex "a little different" from most folks. They also assert they want to help gay children feel good about themselves, give them a positive self-image.

Gay children are said to be subjected to hateful treatment at the hands of other children. They are called cruel names, made fun of, conditioned to feel less than human. And all this abuse is heaped on unfortunate tikes who cannot help being what they are. It is quite a case, enough to make women swoon and hard-hearted men weep with compassion.

But don't get out your "hanky" yet. While many psychiatrists concur that their homosexual patients remember feeling "different" at a very early age, not all psychiatrists agree that feeling of difference is the result of childhood homosexuality. In fact, the homosexuality of an individual in later life may well come from the pre-adolescent feeling of being "different."

Some believe that while the tendency for later sexuality is set at a very early age, it is only the *tendency* and not the fact. We are conditioned to be what we are by environment and upbringing. These two factors have much more to do with what we become than the accident of what we are at birth.

The former homosexual, Guy Charles, told a correspondent for the *National Courier,* "Nobody is born gay. You are born male or female, and the conditioning you receive as you grow up shapes your sexual development. At some point in our lives we make a decision either physically or mentally to participate in a sexual act. The decision is repeated over and over until it's a habit, and the habit forms the life style."

Charles related how he became a homosexual. He was the sickly, anemic son of a Salvation Army bandmaster. His physical progress lagged behind other children his age, but he discovered he had a talent for art. At sixteen he became involved with a well-known designer for the Broadway stage. The man introduced Charles to the practice of homosexuality. Charles was hooked.

Dr. John White in his new book, *Eros Defiled,* tells how in his boyhood in England, a married Christian youth worker introduced him to homosexuality. The man invited young White to spend the weekend at his country place. Strangely, the man insisted White sleep with him while the man's wife slept in the guest room. For two years, the homosexual relationship went on. White was afraid to tell his parents while they continued to encourage him to spend more time with "the nice Christian fellow" who had taken such an unselfish interest in their son. They had no inkling as to why the man was so interested in their boy. White finally overcame the situation, returned to the heterosexual life from which he had been "kidnapped" and is now a Christian counselor and associate professor at the University of Manitoba in Canada.

I do not mean to imply that all homosexuals are child molesters and stealers. They are not. But in a youth conscious age, they are conscious of youth in the extreme and for a very good reason. As the homosexual ages—and particularly, the male homosexual—he begins to lose his appeal to others of his bent. He begins to experience "a nightmare" of rejection. Thus, if he can woo and win the temporary "love" of someone younger, it is a tremendous boost to his ego. Over and over again, in case history after case history, you will find gays stating their first experience was with "an older man" or "older woman."

However, it is not only young people who are wooed by gays. Married men and married women in their middle years have been introduced into homosexual acts by a friend, neighbor or someone they met in a club or bar. Sometimes the new experience is so enticing, the novice will divorce his wife or her husband and take up residence with the gay seducer.

How does it happen? There is, I think, a discernible common thread in all the literally hundreds of case histories I've read or been told while researching this book. Since I am an advertising man by profession, I've come to call it "The Difference Package." And it works the same way all good advertising and sales techniques do.

Now, you will hear a lot these days about how advertising and sales people exert their power by rebuilding value systems and changing the *needs* of consumers. Malarkey. Any ad man worth his salt knows advertising cannot change basic human needs and to attempt it is to waste a great deal of effort and money. What advertising can do is to prevail upon the individual to consider a new and different means of satisfying the basics.

The list of the basic human needs is universal, it applies to both male and female, and it is very short:

1. The need for a relationship with God.
   On most secular lists this is called "The power of the Universe."
2. The need for food.
3. The need for shelter
4. The need for clothing
5. The need for sexual gratification
6. The need to feel uniquely individual
7. The need for happiness
8. The need for friendship
9. The need for security

And that's about it. Depending upon which behaviorist you read, you may find one or two more basic needs listed or one or two less. You may find them arranged in a different order (i.e., some experts persist in placing the need for sexual gratification at the top), but numerical order is misleading anyway since they all cry out within us for satisfaction about equally.

All of your actions all of your life are taken to fulfill one of these basic human needs. The need pattern is unchanging, but how you gratify the needs, and the pattern of secondary wants and desires alter due to conditioning, acceptable social standards, and your station in life.

The wise advertising person, then, spends most of his or her productive time figuring out the exclusive ways in which his client's product or service satisfies the basic human drives: "This toothpaste will give you more sex appeal, because it gives you whiter teeth." "This mouthwash will make more friends for you because it controls bad breath better due to the new XYZ formula." "This car will give you greater security because it has more safety features than any other automobile on the market."

In the advertising business, we call these the "Unique Selling Proposition." In our agency, we sometimes refer to them as "The Appeal Package."

Homosexuals have developed their own USP. It is a pitch which takes advantage of the basic need to feel uniquely individual and couples it with the inferiority complexes we all have in order to create "The Difference Package."

"I felt I was different from the time I was a little girl. I thought I was the only one. Then this woman I met at work asked me to go home with her for dinner one night. She was a lesbian and she helped me to find out that's what I am, too. Now I know why I feel different..."

"I was always different as a boy. Then I read this book about homosexuality. It gave me a name for my difference. Now I think that is what I am...."

"I was always a homosexual. Of course, I didn't realize it until I met another homosexual and he told me what I was..."

Naturally, we all feel different. We all feel we are "the only one" at times. We want to feel different. God made none of us exactly alike. There are many shades in human emotion and feelings and belief. Yet, the homosexual seducer panders to the individual's feeling of being "unique." The seducer then attempts to sell the object of his intention that he was "different" from birth (something to feel good about), and that difference has always been due to a homosexual impulse. Of course, I am over-simplifying the process, but I firmly believe it works just this way in the vast majority of the cases.

The Difference Package as an appeal to young people is dynamite. Adolescence is a terribly confused period in most people's lives. There are drastic hormonal and physical changes taking place, producing strange new emotions and sensations, which heighten the teenager's feeling of being set apart from all others. The process would be hard for the mature mind to understand and cope with; for the immature adolescent it is almost impossible. And when an authoritarian figure comes along—another student, a social worker, a physician, a teacher—and ties all the frustration up in one neat ball and labels it all "homosexuality," the prognosis makes sense, especially to the overly confused child whose body is on the verge of adulthood.

Certainly, there are homosexuals in all professions dealing directly with adolescents who have never influenced youngsters in this manner. Through a doctor friend of mine, I learned of a homosexual physician who "never in all of his long years of practice ever approached a patient." But my doctor friend also told me that this physician was most careful to hide his homosexuality from all but his closest friends. Because of his discretion his young patients do not encounter him thinking, "This is a homosexual first and a doctor second." He is a good role-model as a physician, but he does not try to be a role-model as a homosexual.

The issue with our children is not the hiring of discreet homosexuals, but the forced hiring of publicly declared gays. They want to stand in front of the classroom and say, "I am a homosexual and your teacher."

In the volatile atmosphere of our sex liberated culture the results could be tragic. The booming sex business in our society—pornography, prostitution, etc.—can be attributed, the experts say, to the all pervasive confusion in traditional sex-roles. This same confusion is even more pronounced for today's youth. And as it contributes to the sharp rise in the visibility of pornographic bookstores, massage parlors and street prostitutes, so it contributes to increased visibility and attraction of homosexuality.

"Many feel they are missing something," states a professor in sociology and the behavioral sciences, "after reading all the sexual material in all the media."

And another behaviorist says, "Young people don't want to look, they want to touch."

Young people search out enough taboos on their own without having their adult overseers paint pictures of those taboos for them. And young people want to be part of the action. They don't want to just sit on the sidelines and watch. It is the old story. Children of all ages just don't want to "miss out" on anything that might be good or fun, and forget the consequences.

Generally, too, youngsters tend to believe their teachers and other adults are more intelligent than their own parents. It is always, "But, Dad, my teacher says..." or "That's not right, Mommy, Mrs. Jones told us..." They live with Mom and Dad every day of their lives. The close association lets a child see his parents' strengths and weaknesses, the kinds of things he probably never has a chance to observe in his teachers at school, his scout leader, his clergyman. And because he sees and knows his parents so intimately, it blunts some of their prestige in the child's eyes.

Jesus confirmed this foible's universality when He observed, "A prophet is not without honour, but in his own country, and among his own kin, and in his own house" (Mark 6:4).

The deplorable truth is, today's child spends more time with his teachers and the television set than he does with his own parents in communication. What he doesn't learn from the blackboard in the classroom, he learns from the tube in the family recreation room.

As has been demonstrated, TV is filled with direct references to homosexuality. The fifty-nine specific mentions I monitored in just fourteen hours of viewing in one week's time are only the tip of the iceberg. While all of these were in what would normally be considered "adult" viewing times, we must remember, tonight's "adult" entertainment is frequently next year's afternoon repeat.

My wife and I, like most caring parents, restrict our children's TV habits. We attempt to make certain they watch only those programs we consider "fit" for their consumption. One afternoon, I came home unexpectedly to pick up some office homework I had forgotten to take with me as I rushed from the house in the morning. My wife was attending a meeting. The kids were in the family room with the babysitter watching a half-hour situation comedy which a couple of years before had been heralded as "bold, mature adult entertainment." Yet, in reruns it was being shown in the 3:30 afternoon time slot.

The specific episode they were viewing had to do with the "hilarious" antics of a female impersonator. The big "laugh" just as I came into the family room had to do with the impersonator's entering the men's room.

I turned off the set, fired the babysitter, but the damage had been done. The children were full of questions which I attempted to answer to the best of my ability. I tried, too, to make them understand what the Bible has to say about such matters.

In a way, I felt sorry for the babysitter. She is a good Christian woman. She had gotten too wrapped up in her reading to pay much attention to what the children were seeing on television. As she said to me through her tears, "I'm sorry, Mr. Rodgers, but I thought if they put it on in the middle of the afternoon it would be all right for youngsters."

The real culprit was not the babysitter, although she was lax in her duties; the real culprits were the television executives who scheduled the program at that early hour. And it was not the local station, but the network.

There is something hypocritical about a system of programming which talks about a "family hour" and does its level best to keep adult viewing matter scheduled away from the time period, while at the same time scheduling mature programs at the very hour when children are most likely to be viewing.

Ironic, too, that parents and social institutions, including the church, are organizing to protest the amount of violence on television without protesting the volume of prurient materials made available to the young and unsophisticated.

But, maybe we are so saturated with the sewage which passes as "serious" drama, maybe we have been so assaulted by murder and mayhem, that anything—*anything*—without gunfire and bloodshed and screams in the night is a welcome change of pace. After all, every man, woman, boy and girl in the U.S. now spends more time watching television than they spend doing anything else, except sleeping! That unbelievable statistic was given to me by one of the sales executives for a local television station. It was taken from a reputable national survey.

Where are we going?

England has been down the path before us. In 1967, the English Parliament passed the Sex Offenses Act which permits homosexual practices by consenting adults defined as anyone 21 years of age or older.

Since then, England has been described as "the gayest country in the world. A homosexual paradise on earth."

Groups of active and militant gays have been allowed to address children in public schools. School children there have also been taken to a theatrical workshop in London to participate in something called the "Gay Sweatshop." Comprised of professional gay actors and using the facilities of a theatre in central London, the "Gay Sweatshop" puts on plays expressing the difficulties faced by homosexuals. The day-long program consists of two parts. In the morning the pupils are asked to participate in improvised plays, psycho dramas, and discussion groups centered around the theme of "feeling different." This is supposed to let the individual heterosexual youngster identify with the special condition of being homosexual; to let him or her feel the good points as well as the bad. In the afternoon, the pupils are treated to the professionally performed "entertainments" about homosexuality.

No wonder English parents, members of Parliament and scrupulous educators are calling upon the British Prime Minister to stop the "growing exploitation" by gays of the British school child. They acknowledge the decline of public and private morals in Britain during the past decade.

If liberalization and decriminalization of homosexuality have not worked in England, if they have had such a ruinous effect there, how can we expect it to be any different here?

The Gay Invasion is worldwide in scope. In Greece, homosexuals march for "human rights." In France, in Holland, in South America, in a dozen other countries the chant is the same, "Gay is proud. Give us your children. Let us show them there is nothing to fear."

If only adults suffered by it and through it, it might be easier to cope with. At least adults should be old enough and wise enough to fend for themselves. But it is the children who will suffer, who are suffering.

In Washington D.C. and in several states in this country, avowed homosexuals cannot be denied the right of adopting children so long as they are otherwise of "good character." Courts have granted the right to lesbian mothers to retain custody of children from their previous heterosexual marriages, even though those mothers now live with their same-sex lovers.

And, as if it wasn't enough, there is a report that lesbians who want children are seeking artificial insemination. There is even an organization operating under the banner, "Lesbian Mothers Union."

One little boy was encouraged to call his mother's female lover, "Daddy." Other lesbians have been named foster parents and even operated foster homes. One transsexual during his pre-operative treatment was allowed to be a foster parent to a number of children.

Homosexuals drag their children to meetings of Gay Liberation. They openly embrace, and hug and hold hands in front of them. As one said, "I don't want my child to have any preconception about what is 'normal' and what is not."

But the Lord God says, "Ye shall not afflict any widow, or fatherless child. If thou afflict them in any wise, and they

124

cry at all unto me, I will surely hear their cry; And my wrath shall wax hot, and I will kill you with the sword..." (Exodus 22:22-24).

That judgment, as much as it is on those who would "afflict" children with their unnaturalness, is upon us who would tolerate it. We are to protect the children who are unable to protect themselves. We cannot stand by and see this thing come to pass which evil men would perpetrate upon us in the name of reasonable enlightenment. There is nothing reasonable or enlightened about sin.

A college in a large metropolitan center has a class on Inner City dynamics. One of the instructors is a professed homosexual. For the final examination in this class, the students are asked to dress in old clothing, take only one dollar with them, and to live on the streets for six days without going home. It is a course in street survival and is supposed to acquaint the students with the underprivileged, the alcoholics, the dropouts of life. The class members are told to seek out gay members of the opposite sex and attempt to find lodging with them, because they are "safe."

The students are young, in their early twenties for the most part. One girl described her days and nights on the street. She described visiting gay bars; how she went home with a lesbian for a meal; how she spent the nights wandering the streets of the city. She talked of two male gays who befriended her and bought her coffee in an all-night restaurant. She told of being threatened in the parking lot of a fast-food chain by a gay guy in female dress when he thought she was making a "pass" at another male homosexual.

I have heard these reports and am appalled that a city college and instructors in that college could ask students to do something so potentially dangerous and morally degrading.

And what do the students learn? To accept the outlandish lifestyle of overt homosexuals. They come away I think, in many instances, with more misconceptions about homosexuals and gay stereotypes than if they had never been "on the gays' turf."

But, you know, it is "good" strategy on the part of gay

educators. If students learn to deal with exaggerated homosexual behavior, how much more acceptable will be the behavior of "ordinary homosexuals." Yes, good strategy for the gays, but a massacre of young people's morals.

College students are not children in the strictest sense of the word, but they are young and they are extremely impressionable and usually unguarded when it comes to idealogies espoused by those who teach them.

My father has always said, "It takes eight years for a young person to get over a college education." And he's not anti-higher education. He forced me to go to a university for a minimum of two years. He knew that once I had finished my sophomore year, I would probably stick around to complete the remaining two years for a Bachelor of Arts. Smart man, my father. But with the status of higher education today, I wonder if his eight year timetable is enough.

I was discussing some of the material in this chapter with several of the leaders in the suburban community in which I reside. "What is wrong with all that?" one woman asked. "I'd like my children to learn about those things and the earlier the better. I want them to know the options open to them. I mean, it is better than the drug scene of the last few years."

The world is full of them, stage mothers and fathers. And, not only in the theatre.

11
Devil's Nightmare, Satan's Blinders

You and your spouse sit in the cozy living room. A fire crackles and pops in the fireplace. In the corner, the television set plays merrily away. You are happy, contented. Even the evening newspaper carries nothing but good news for a change.

Then, suddenly, you are aware of your teenage son. He has come into the room without your noticing. He stands there, a strapping, handsome hunk of a teenager. You are so proud of him, and yet...

Tonight there is something about him...something you can't quite put your finger on...something unsettling...something strange...something unreal...

"Mom? Dad? Could we talk?" You're relieved that the voice that speaks is his voice. A moment ago, he seemed almost demonic.

You relax and smile.

"Well?" he asks.

You nod and he settles on the couch, but not in the disjointed sprawl you are accustomed to seeing. His posture is rigid, tense.

You put your paper down and come to the edge of your chair. There is a long silence.

"You wanted to have a little talk?" you hear yourself finally saying.

"Yes," he says solemnly in a way that causes a little chill to run up your spine. "What I have to say is heavy. Real heavy. So please, just don't say anything 'til I've laid it out."

You agree, exchanging anxious glances with your spouse.

"You guys have always been great parents. Like you've always been a lot more 'hip' than lots of kids' folks," he begins.

You know you've been paid a compliment and should acknowledge it. But before you can clear your throat he goes on...

"And I know this isn't gonna' go down as heavy with you as a lot of other people, but..." His voice trails away, and then he is on his feet, pacing.

"But what?" you prompt.

"I don't know an easy way to say it," he says, "so, I guess I'll just lay it on you. You read the papers, watch the tube. You know there's a certain kind of person that's like—different. You know, I mean like, really different. They're homo—gays."

You clutch.

"And you know Hal. He's like my best friend. And, well, he's... he's gay."

The tightness in your chest and throat moderate. You sigh. He wants to talk to you about a friend of his; he wants help in dealing with something he does not understand.

"That's a shame, son," you intend to say, but before you can open your mouth he has stopped you with a look you find unbearable.

"This is probably gonna' blow your skull," he's saying, "and I'm sorry. I really am. But, I'm..."

"NO!" you scream, sitting bolt upright in bed.

The images are gone. The house is dark, quiet. Your spouse stirs but does not awaken. The crickets chirp outside the bedroom window.

In a cold sweat, you throw back the covers and climb out of bed. Tiptoeing down the unlighted hallway, you peek into your son's room. He's asleep in his bed. The moonlight catches the football pennants thumbtacked to the wall and bounces off the glass in the picture frame enclosing the smiling countenance of his steady girl friend on the night table.

You stand for a long while listening to the sound of his deep, regular slumber. Oh, how you love that boy. At last, satisfied, you gently pull shut his door and go back to your bed.

Sleep is slow in returning. You lay there hearing the little creaks and groans of your house; the normal sounds of the night.

Normal. How reassuring that word is. And you say a small

prayer of thanksgiving that it was only a dream, a nightmare whose unreality was all too real momentarily. And you know it will slowly fade from your consciousness, and yet, it will never be wholly forgotten.

Your bad dream will fade. But for all too many parents, this devil's nightmare is unending. They are the mothers and fathers of children who have declared themselves homosexual.

The reactions are as varied as the parents to whom it has happened. One mother is reported to have written her gay son a letter telling him: "Don't ever call or write us again. Stay away from your brothers and sisters. If I ever see you on the street, it will make me sick."

A father said, "At first we didn't know how to deal with Linda's lesbianism. But now her lover is just like our son's wives. She's a lovely girl. Our family circle wouldn't be complete without her."

Another parent told a writer, "It's like having a child who's diabetic, or slightly retarded, or with a physical deformity—a child a little out of the 'norm.' Every one of us is a little out of the ordinary, so what makes a gay different?"

A gay is different because his is not an illness, or a mental handicap. It is a handicap of the soul. But that is sometimes hard for a parent to see.

And regardless of their final conclusions about their off-spring's gayness, all parents confronted by it report the same basic reaction: guilt—"What did we do wrong?"

People have been so brainwashed by the theories of Freud and his disciples that they believe a homosexual has to be the result of faulty upbringing. They know it just has to be the fault of the parents. And sometimes it is.

A mother has always wanted a daughter, but when she has a son, she tries to make him a substitute for her desires. She encourages him to play with dolls. She dresses him in soft, feminine-type clothing. She takes him to the beauty parlor with her. She teaches him the games of girls.

A father who has always wanted a son, but is denied, encourages his daughter to participate in sports, or other masculine activities. He never buys her a dress, unless forced to do so by his wife, but showers his daughter with T-shirts and ball caps and catcher's mitts. He rewards her for achievements in the male domain and ignores or rejects her when she does something a girl would do normally.

Obviously, in both instances, there is a potential for ultimate homosexuality in the child. But a "sissy boy," or a female "tomboy" does not necessarily grow up to be gay. They can be as heterosexual in their identity as any other individual. And, usually, the cases in which parents contribute to the homosexuality of a son or daughter are not nearly as melodramatic. For often the only action a parent takes is really "inaction."

One young gay says, "If only my father had taken me to a ball game or on a camping trip. If only he had done something with me just once while I was growing up, things might have turned out differently."

His father was preoccupied with business. He was a dynamic community leader. He was constantly on the go to one committee meeting after the other. He loved his son, but had no time for him. He begat the sinner and reaped his grief.

My friend Brice once said to me, "My father doesn't understand my interest in theatre. It's like I live on another planet. He's always telling me to be tougher, more ruthless. He wants me to be 'a man.' If he only knew. But you know what? I don't think he'd care."

I think Brice wanted his father's support in the worst way. Outside the physical and material things of life, I don't think he ever got it. Was that why Brice became a homosexual? It is probably not the only reason, but I would imagine it had something to do with it.

Then there are fathers like Bud. Bud is the super-sportsman in one of the neighborhoods we used to live in and the father of identical twin boys. Bud isn't content to just encourage his sons—he drives them, hard. He is constantly insisting they perform feats of athletic prowess which no preadolescent boys with twice the twins' ability could accomplish. When they fall short of the goal Bud has set for them—and that is almost constantly because the goals are so outrageous to begin with—

he makes fun of them pitilessly. The kids always walk around with a "hang-dog" look. You can almost see the cloud of failure over their heads.

Ethel, Bud's wife, doesn't help matters either. She counters Bud's mania for manliness by smothering the twins with comfort. If Bud tells the boys to do something, Ethel will invariably order them not to do it. The poor kids are pushed and pulled this way and that in the unending battle of parental wills.

Given what some experts report to be a high incidence of homosexuality in twins—one source places it as high as one out of every three—with Bud's ridicule and Ethel's smothering, it should surprise no one if one or both twins turns out gay.

Fathers can play a big role in rearing homosexual daughters, too. Peter and Barbara Wyden in their book, *Growing Up Straight: What Every Thoughtful Parent Should Know About Homosexuality* (Stein & Day), considered by some to be a "classic," say: "The fathers [of lesbians] tend to be unusually puritanical, to engender fear (not necessarily physical) in their daughters, to belittle the daughter's male and female friends, to ally with the daughter against her mother, and to discourage feminine dress, dancing, and the use of make-up."

This statement seems to be aimed squarely at some fundamental Christians. But reading between the lines, I think it has nothing to do with whether a father bans dancing, immodest dress or makeup. I think the important thing is how it is done. It is vital for a father to treat his daughter with love and understanding. If he is strict with her, she must know it is being done out of concern for her physical and spiritual well-being.

In addition, fathers and mothers should be aware, but not overly so, of some of the symptoms of a predisposition towards homosexuality. The Doctors Bieber, a husband and wife team —he is a psychiatrist, she a clinical psychologist— listed some of the classic signals of impending gayness in a newspaper article. They are:

- The child dislikes group play, preferring to do things alone or with his mother.
- The child is excessively afraid of physical injury.

- The child, if male, finds his father overtly hostile or indifferent to him.
- The child adopts the mannerisms of the opposite sex—as, for instance, when a boy in his early teens imitates the walk of a girl.

I cannot stress enough that parents should not overly react to these symptoms. In the child with a real homosexual proclivity, more than one is almost always present. And children do go through stages. For example, my own son for several years was extremely frightened of physical injury. He did not want to play football because he was afraid he might get hurt. He did not want to join the army, when he grew up, he said, because he was afraid he might get maimed or killed.

Interestingly enough, at the time he was going through this phase, the war in Vietnam was in full swing. The nightly news reports were bloody and graphic. While we tried to keep him from seeing too many of these, I think those he did happen to watch frightened him. But he outgrew the fear and is now so rough and tumble, it scares me.

Yes, parents must be careful about reacting too quickly. The same article which reported the Biebers' list of homosexual symptoms also pointed out that it is extremely difficult for even the most inept parents to turn their heterosexual child gay. If the symptoms are detected, I think I would wait until I was absolutely certain that it was not just some phase my child was going through, and then I would quietly and discreetly seek good Christian professional help. I would not alert the child that I was concerned. To do so might cause the child to doubt his or her own sexuality. It might lead them to conclude, "If my folks are worried I am a homosexual, then I must be one."

The greatest danger posed by the Gay Invasion is "gay phobia." Evidence of this is already being observed. Parents worry if their children are not *supra-heterosexual* at an early age. Young people worry if they are not overly attracted to members of the opposite sex very early in life. They worry that they might be homosexual, and sometimes tragically arrive at the conclusion they are, without ever having experienced a real homosexual thought other than their own fear. Psychologists call such individuals, "pseudohomosexuals."

But what happens when the fears prove true? What should a parent's reaction be?

Homosexuals and their sympathizers say the best course is "a complete and positive acceptance."

When a twenty-year-old man confessed his gayness to his devout Christian mother, she immediately took him to a psychiatrist. She was reportedly not worried about his homosexuality. Her sole question to the doctor was, "Can he be homosexual and happy?"

That is like asking, "Can he be an alcoholic and happy?" It depends on your point-of-view. But we place a great importance on "happiness" in our world today. Too frequently, when we say happy, we mean "well-adjusted" to the human condition. We mean wealth and euphoria. What we really should be concerned about is if our child will be "God-adjusted."

Oddly, in most published cases, the parents seldom seek help from their ministers. Most say they would be too "ashamed."

"My minister is too rock-hard," a mother told me. "He would never understand. He'd just quote the Bible. I've read the Bible and all that it has to say on the subject. I want help, not condemnation. My [child]... isn't a Frankenstein, he isn't a leper. He's just my little boy."

Some ministers are unprepared to deal with homosexuality. But a minister who bases his counsel on solid Biblical-foundations, who advises in Christian love, can offer so much more than if the parent tries to "go it alone."

There are some pastors, conversely, who are all too willing to counsel on homosexuality. They are those who would liberalize the interpretation of God's law. They subscribe to what Guy Charles has labeled "gay theology." They misinterpret the love of Christ for the love of man.

Although I never discussed homosexuality with him, I once knew a minister who said, "You kids raised in the Christian tradition don't know what life is all about. You won't be any good until you roll in the gutter." He would probably applaud a gay relationship as a necessary maturing in the process of

Christian love.

Paul set a good example for the Christian minister and the Christian counselor. He wrote, "I write not these things to shame you, but as my beloved sons I warn you" (I Corinthians 4:14). That should be the motive of any Christian who speaks out against homosexuality.

And it should be in the hearts of every parent confronted by a gay son or daughter. The same parent who would never dream of abandoning his child to alcoholism or to a serious and debilitating killer-disease, the same parent who would do everything in his power to get his child to give up narcotics, will surrender that child to a homosexual lifestyle.

The parents may pray for awhile, they may cry out like Job: "How many are mine iniquities and sins? Make me to know my transgression and my sin" (Job 13:23). But when their prayer isn't instantly answered to their satisfaction, when God does not beat them over the head with the mistakes they made in rearing their offspring, they quit praying and quit asking. "Well, if it is going to be that way," they say, "it's going to be."

They may turn to an organization like "Parents of Gays," a group whose founder is quoted as counseling, "The past is the past. It's much more effective not to ask, 'Why did this happen?' but to ask, 'What can I do now to help him or her?' —to devote energy to the present. Once people believe that homosexuality is a variation on human sexuality, it loses its negative connotation."

Or, they may work it out totally on their own. They may arrive at such complete acceptance of homosexuality that their child's same-sex lover is included at all family functions. They are invited for holidays and weddings and birthdays.

A lesbian said she knew her family had come to grips with her condition when they expressed disappointment over the fact that her lover had gone to spend Christmas with her, the lover's, own relatives.

Pastors of the gay Metropolitan Community Churches boast that within their congregations are parents of homosexuals who have joined the church, bringing with them their other children, thus demonstrating their acceptance of their gay child's sexual inversion.

"It is better that his mother and I learn to live with his homosexuality," says a father, "than to lose him."

Would this same father say, "Better he lose his soul than for us to lose a son?" I think not. But that is exactly what he is saying.

Whether parents eagerly accept their child's gayness or whether they reject it or completely ignore it by avoiding any stand pro or con, they are wearing Satan's blinders.

Blinders are the flaps sewn to a horse's bridle in a way that keeps him from seeing to either side or behind him. All the horse can see are those things directly in front of him. The idea is to keep his concentration on the road ahead, to keep him from getting nervous and skitterish over peripheral distractions—bushes stirred by a gentle breeze, a bird flushed from the weeds at the side of the trail, that kind of thing. Blinders are most often used on race horses and on horses pulling wagons. It keeps them from paying too much attention to the horses beside them. But sometimes a pair of blinders is required on a saddle horse.

Satan's blinders keep us moving straight, too. Straight down the "smooth" path and over the edge to perdition.

The parents of homosexuals are not supposed to be accessories to sin. They are not to wear the same blinders their children wear. They are not to join in forging the Great Lie of acceptability that makes unholiness holy.

The same chapter of the book of Romans which refers to lesbianism ends with this verse: "Who knowing the judgment of God, that they which commit such things are worthy of death, not only do the same, but have pleasure in them that do them" (Romans 1:32).

There are two thoughts here, I think. First, those who know and are aware that God's Word prohibits a specific act, and yet go ahead and perform the act, are worthy of death; death not only by dying but by the living death of eternal punishment. And, second, those who know God's law and yet encourage others to break that law are as bad, if not worse than the actual transgressors. They are joined and considered as one-in-the-same in God's eyes.

The parent who knows God's way in the matter cannot hold his silence just because it is more convenient or less abrasive to the parent-child relationship. The fourth chapter of Second Timothy begins with a passage which teaches us exactly what the nature of the Christian role should be in dealing with wrongdoers. While the instruction is not aimed at parents in particular, it is good advice for parents, nonetheless. It says, "I charge thee therefore before God, and the Lord Jesus Christ, who shall judge the quick and the dead at his appearing and his kingdom; preach the word; be instant in season, out of season; reprove, rebuke, exhort with all longsuffering and doctrine. For the time will come when they will not endure sound doctrine; but after their own lusts shall they heap to themselves teachers, having itching ears; and they shall turn away their ears from the truth, and shall be turned unto fables" (II Timothy 4:1-4).

I particularly like the way in which Zondervan's *Amplified Bible* translates the last portion of this passage, "And will turn aside from hearing the truth and wander off into myths and man-made fictions."

That is an apt description of the self-justifying homosexual, isn't it?

However, before you get too carried away with your preaching, remember, preaching is not only loud proclamation with a little hyperbole thrown in, it can also be instruction and urging with quiet earnestness.

There was a television commercial for a perfume company in which a beautiful woman addressed the camera in a whisper saying, "If you want to get someone's attention, whisper..."

I don't know what the actual viewership statistics for that particular commercial were, but I would imagine they were quite high. The first time the commercial ran, many people probably did a double take wondering whether their television set was on the fritz because the usual blare and blast was muted. I would guess it even brought a few people back to their television sets from the kitchen where they had gone to get a drink of water while the commercials were on.

Yes, quietness can get more rapt attention than noise and bluster, especially with one's own family. The Bible advises, "A soft answer turneth away wrath: but grievous words stir up anger" (Proverbs 15:1).

Going back to Second Timothy, in the King James version, verse five of the Scripture continues, "But watch thou in all things, endure afflictions, do the work of an evangelist, make full proof of thy ministry."

In other words, "Keep your cool. Be persistent but patient." For there is no question that children of any stripe can surely try a parent's endurance, and how much more so the homosexual son or daughter.

"You have no idea. We made a real attempt with her. We did," said her father with tears in his eyes. "But the sickness of her mind, the wickedness of her thoughts were too much. The more we tried, the worse she got. She refused to see that it [homosexuality] was a bad thing. The arguments we had got more heated.

"Then, last Memorial Day—and I'll never forget it—she stormed out of the house. We let her go. I figured it was either lose our minds," he put his arm around his wife, "or our daughter. She's been gone a long time now. If she ever comes back . . ."

He didn't finish. His hostility and bitterness boiled within. He had lost all patience.

But patience is a prerequisite of good parenthood. Look at the parable of the prodigal son in Luke 15. It is a story so well-known that we'll not repeat it here. But the father in the tale did some things every father and every mother, too, would do well to emulate when dealing with immorality in their children: he was patient beyond endurance and he kept the door open for a possible return. When the boy did come back, the father was ready to meet and accept him with forgiveness.

While Jesus didn't say as He related the story, there is strong indication that the father's character was such that he probably did something else. He probably prayed.

As James says, "The effectual fervent prayer of a righteous

man availeth much" (James 5:16).

Thus, there are four things a parent can do when faced with a son or daughter who announces their homosexuality. Persevere. Pray. Preach. Endure with patience.

Persevere against the man-made myths which would have you accept your child's homosexuality as a reasonable variation of the norm.

Pray that God will help to turn your child from his sin; and give you power to do your part.

Preach, that is, instruct your child in righteousness using the Bible as your guide. Learn the truth about homosexuality and teach your child that truth.

Endure with patience, that is, don't expect sudden miracles. They do occur sometimes, but not often. Keep the door to reconciliation open. Be ready to forgive, if your child is ready to repent.

But can homosexuals really be cured? Can they really become heterosexuals?

Or is that notion just more of the same: The devil's nightmare, Satan's blinders?

12
"Gay Liberation" a Good Thing?

Can homosexuality be "cured?" Can the gay individual be liberated from his or her plight?

Over the centuries, man has tried mightily to "reclaim" homosexuals from their abnormality. The techniques employed have not always been humane or even rational. And always their rate of success or failure has been hotly contended.

In the early nineteenth century, homosexuality was considered lunacy and the practitioners of sodomy were, when caught, promptly committed to a lunatic asylum where they were chained in their own filth, beaten and dehumanized entirely. Few ever emerged from these dark chambers of horror with their sanity completely intact.

Toward the middle of the 1800s, medical people began to realize that homosexuality was not necessarily degenerate insanity and started to use more moderate treatments. One physician treated a lesbian patient, for example, with cold sitz baths and "a course of intellectual treatment." He boasted a cure, although, a later analysis of her case history indicated there had been none.

Sigmund Freud tried to treat homosexuality by analyzing a patient's dreams and exploring the subconscious. This was done in order to bring the individual face-to-face with his guilt and the motivations for the thoughts and actions leading to that guilt. By facing these, the patient was supposed to be able to better deal with his mental sickness; his neurosis and psychosis. Freud's emphasis was not really on "cure" as much as it was on making a person feel good about himself by eliminating his guilt feelings. To accomplish this, Freud preached permissiveness in all things, especially sex. His concern was to make his patients "happy," rather than "healed."

Some physicians have tried to cure homosexuality through radical surgical mutilation of the body's sexual members in an effort to eliminate the cause of "powerful urgings." By-and-large, this method failed, as did repeated attempts to normalize the brain by performing lobotomies. A lobotomy is a highly complex procedure in which a lobe of the brain is cut into or across. The idea is to sever nerve fibers which supply signals upon which the individual acts. "In layman's terms, it is rather like disconnecting some of the circuits in a computer," a physician said.

The lobotomy is a highly risky surgical method and in the homosexual has often done more harm than good.

Other doctors have dealt with homosexuality as a genetic and endocrinal disorder. They have injected large doses of hormones into their subjects. Others have used chemicals to produce shocks to the nervous system and thus stun the patient into normalcy. In 1940, a physician from Atlanta, Georgia reported success in treating homosexuals with a chemical stimulant that produced convulsive shock. But his success has not been duplicated since.

In more recent times, electroshock has been tried. As in chemical shock, the object is to create convulsive seizures designed to change a subject's behavior patterns. But in this case, the convulsions are manufactured by electric current. Success in curing the homosexual is said to be temporary, if a cure is effected at all.

Psychotherapists today use many of the techniques first pioneered by Freud. Through conversational interchange, they try to draw the patient out of himself. They examine his most intimate thoughts in detail and analyze each with him. In this process they try to give the patient "insight" into his psychological problems and thereby help him to discover just why it is he or she prefers the same sex over the opposite sex.

Frequently, hypnosis comes into play. The subject is placed in a trance and given subconscious suggestions which are anti-homosexual and pro-heterosexual in nature. For example, the subject might be told to visualize his same-sex lover as covered with sores and reeking with an offensive odor. Then the hypnotist calls to mind the image of the opposite sex which is hypnotically associated with beauty and pleasant perfumes.

To my mind, the trouble with hypnosis is that it gives a man dominion over our thoughts when our focus should be upon our God. Some Christian therapists, however, claim that in the "right" hands (Christian hands), it can be a powerful tool for healing. I have my doubts as a layman.

Another technique psychotherapists use is called "Aversion Therapy." They show pictures of the same and opposite sexes to the gay under treatment. When the pictures of his same sex are shown, pain by electric shock or illness induced by drugs is applied. Conversely, when pictures of the opposite sex are flashed before him, he is made to feel pleasant. Sometimes he is given relaxing drugs and sometimes soft, soothing music is played. Eventually, when the process is repeated over and over, the homosexual is supposed to get violently ill whenever he has a gay thought, and feel sublimely happy whenever he has a heterosexual one. If he is male, men are therefore not supposed to be attractive to him, while his sexual attraction to women is encouraged.

There are successes with all of these techniques. But there are also monumental failures. The therapists have a tendency to rationalize their washouts with the explanation: "In order for the cure to work, the homosexual has to want to change."

The sad fact is, according to the experts, that most homosexuals definitely do not want to give up being gay. Surveys among homosexuals show that ninety to ninety-six percent of them would not want to change to heterosexuals even if they could be given "some magic sex shot," or push "a magic button" which would reverse their sexual orientation without pain or suffering.

It is interesting, too, that about the same number of practicing gays say that while they do not want to change, they would not wish the lifestyle for anyone else. That is hard to believe in light of the Gay Liberation movement now so vocal in our society.

Yet it remains that man's attempt to cure homosexuality through medical or psychological means has been largely abortive. In the seventies, the American Psychiatric Association apparently decided to give up altogether, for they declared that "homosexuality" was no longer classed as an illness and removed the word entirely from their *Standard Diagnostic Manual.*

They were right, but I think for the wrong reasons.

You see, if we continue to talk about homosexuality as a "sickness," then we have to find a "cure." The problem is defining what "cure" means. Does it mean simply healing the individual of his homosexual desires? Or does it mean changing the individual's practice from homosexual to heterosexual? There is a great difference.

Some experts used to recommend heterosexual marriage to their gay patients as "the sure cure." Unfortunately, such a marriage was undertaken for the improper purpose. It was a selfish purpose. True Christian marriage is based upon selflessness. It is a sharing of souls. Of course, the "curative marriages" were doomed almost without exception, if not to divorce, to destruction. How many spouses of gays and children of these unions were sentenced to suffering in the name of healing?

More prudent behaviorists never recommend marriage to the homosexual, unless they are convinced that the individual has indeed undergone a metamorphosis in desire and deed.

Neither do I believe the current approach in modern medical and behavioral circles any more valid. I am speaking of the practice which undertakes a cure of the homosexual's mental and emotional problems while leaving his basic gay identity undisturbed, or even reinforcing it.

An article published by one psychiatrist in a medical journal told how he was often able to help individuals "find their homosexuality." He said that when these patients came to him, they did not realize they were gay. They thought their problems were normal sexual dysfunctions. But he was able to enlighten them to their suppressed homosexuality and to aid them in establishing their "true sexual identity."

"But ye are forgers of lies, ye are all physicians of no value" (Job 13:4).

142

However, not all therapists are "forgers of lies." Some like Dr. Samuel B. Hadden have formed therapeutic groups for homosexuals. He has written much on the subject. He says, "One of the beneficial effects observed is the speed with which the group breaks down the rationalization of its component members. It becomes quite apparent that the smug rationalizations are a faulty protection against the intense anxiety which exists about their abnormality. In such groups, discussion of the... high suicide rate, the loneliness and the ostracism that these individuals must eventually face are soon brought to the fore, and discussion along these lines quickly demonstrates that even those who have avowed that they wish to be nothing more than insatiable homosexuals soon have their rationalizations shattered, and then seek to change to a normal pattern of behavior."

Dr. Hadden has also written, "There is no question that the treatment of homosexuality leaves much to be desired. To accept it as a hopeless condition, however, will not contribute to the solution of the problem or add to the state of happiness of future generations of homosexuals, even though laws are modified to their wishes..."

Why does the treatment leave "much to be desired"? Why aren't more homosexuals anxious to become normal? Why aren't more homosexuals cured?

Because "cure" talks about "illness," and not even the American Psychiatric Association talks about homosexuality in that light anymore. The question is not, "Can homosexuality be cured?" but rather, "Can homosexuals be redeemed?"

And that asks, "Can homosexuals be *liberated* from their sin?"

Yes. By Jesus Christ.

"For the wages of sin is death, but the gift of God is eternal life through Jesus Christ, our Lord" (Romans 6:23). To have eternal life means to be cleansed from all unrighteousness. In God's sight. And the believer in Christ becomes a new creation; old things are gone and he has a new life, according to II Corinthians 5:17.

But we must understand the complete nature of the deliver-

143

ance. In all too many cases, Christians look for an immediate, dramatic turnabout; an instant cessation of all former temptations and lusts. And yes, sometimes—praise God—it happens just that way. Sometimes, but not always.

When I was still in the broadcasting business, I had the opportunity to witness to an aging homosexual. He made no pretense about his sexual habits, but age had made him begin to question himself. He was searching for "the something" more in life.

He was a member of the staff at a studio where I did some freelance announcing on occasion and we had known each other in a casual working relationship for some time. But why he sought me out for a discussion of his philosophies, I do not know. Maybe he sensed in me the stability and concern for others that most Christians have as a result of walking with our God and our Lord.

There are two kinds of active Christian witnesses. There are those who aggressively ask everyone they know, everyone they meet, everyone they happen to pass on a crowded street, "Are you saved?" And while I admire these people when they are sincere, such is not my calling. I belong to the second group of witnesses. I witness unto others by living my life as an example to them. At least, I try. It is amazing how many opportunities to share the gospel come to those who watch and wait patiently for them.

The aging homosexual was one of my opportunities. I asked him if he had seen a pastor for advice and counsel.

"Oh, no," he said. "A preacher would just want to save me."

"Well, you could do a lot worse," I said.

"Listen, kid, I tried religion once. I even went down front during one of those big crusades. They prayed over me and talked with me and gave me some literature to read. I walked out of there thinking, 'Hallelujah, I've found it.' I was determined that I wasn't gonna' sin anymore. But not two days later, I was 'tempted' as you Christians say. Religion just didn't work for me."

Of course, it can be argued that his was a spurious conversion experience. But I'm only reporting here a brief excerpt of a conversation which lasted several hours. I am convinced that his profession of faith was genuine. It was his expectation which was false.

From the day we are born, we are subject to the temptations of the flesh and the devil. It is not important to this discussion to understand all the reasons why Satan tempts us. Suffice it to say, he is at war with God.

Man is the casualty, because the nature of his flesh allows him to tempt himself. Satan does not have to do all the work, he waits for or uses our self-temptation to open the door to his purpose.

But why temptation for a Christian? What possible good can come from it? Why does temptation continue to be a problem for a Christian after he has come to the cross?

The book of James explains it thusly, "My brethren, count it all joy when ye fall into divers temptations; knowing this, that the trying of your faith worketh patience. But let patience have her perfect work, that ye may be perfect and entire, wanting nothing.

"Blessed is the man that endureth temptation: for when he is tried, he shall receive the crown of life, which the Lord hath promised to them that love him" (James 1:2-4 and 12).

Temptation, you see, does have a purpose. It serves to strengthen our faith. And Christians especially are not denied the privilege of temptation, for it builds confidence in our saved condition.

That is why acceptance of God's plan of salvation does not necessarily remove former stumbling blocks completely and immediately from our lives. What it does do, is to give us the power to overcome them.

Turning from the practice of homosexuality may be a protracted and agonizing experience. Guy Charles told a reporter who interviewed him that it took a year and a half for him to be "healed" of his homosexuality once he had given his life completely to the Lord. He stumbled and fell, but, according to the published interview, "The Lord brought me around so gently, so lovingly," Charles said.

Theologians far more wise than I point out there is a difference between *"being tempted* of homosexuality" and *"practicing* homosexualism." We have little choice in our base urgings, they say, but we can control how we respond to our impulses.

A psychiatrist interviewed on radio about suicide said, "There is no such thing as an uncontrollable impulse. The same muscles which pick up the gun can stop you from pulling the trigger."

Homosexuals who continue to practice homosexuality are committing moral suicide. They are killing their souls. God can give them the spiritual muscles to stop pulling the trigger.

Temptation keeps us honest. It keeps us humble. It keeps us grateful for the new life that is ours through the blood of Jesus. And, thank God that when we do yield to the temptation, He has promised to forgive us if we are sorry for our sin and confess it to Him (I John 1:9).

But gays have a tendency to believe that theirs is a very special kind of case. They often excuse their actions by such belief. They preach that homosexuality is only one kind of sin, no better or worse than any other kind of sin, but they fail to realize that it is also just another kind of temptation, no better or worse than any other kind of temptation.

Although we are tempted, God does not intend temptation to be an excuse to keep on sinning. The problem is, many homosexuals refuse to recognize their sexual urgings as sin, at all. Encouraged by liberal churchmen, they come to look upon it as a gift.

"I used to believe that gayness was temptation," one homosexual has said, "and when I came to Christ I thought I would never be tempted again. But I was and am. I prayed about it and when the temptation did not go away, I came to the conclusion that He must want me to remain as I am. It must be His gift to me as heterosexuality is His gift to you."

The homosexual is practicing self-delusion who says this to himself. The Bible clearly says that we are never "tempted of God" (James 1:13; see also verses 14-16). "God cannot be tempted of evil, neither tempteth he any man...."

Since sin is evil, and God cannot abide evil, would He give that evil to one of His children as a "gift?" Absolutely not!

A homosexual may earnestly believe he has been born with the tendency to be gay. But to justify his continued slavery to it by naming it "a gift," is simply one more way of avoiding confrontation with the will of the flesh.

And we are warned, "Let not sin therefore reign in your mortal body, that ye should obey it in the lusts thereof. Neither yield ye your members as instruments of unrighteousness unto sin: but yield yourselves unto God, as those that are alive from the dead, and your members as instruments of righteousness unto God. For sin shall not have dominion over you: for ye are not under the law, but under grace" (Romans 6:12-14).

Homosexual temptation is no reason for continuing homosexual acts. We are promised, "There hath no temptation taken you but such as is common to man: but God is faithful, who will not suffer you to be tempted above that ye are able; but will with the temptation also make a way to escape, that ye may be able to bear it" (I Corinthians 10:13).

In Christ, we will not be tempted beyond our means to endure.

There is a great fallacy in the homosexual community that the only person who can help a gay is another gay or one who has been gay. But as we can see, the trouble is *not* homosexuality per se, it is *temptation*. And temptation is something we can all understand because we have all been tempted, heterosexual and homosexual alike.

But the erroneous belief persists and effectively bars the "way to escape" for many homosexuals who would. If I was a homosexual and wanted to make a bona fide attempt to change my life, the first thing I would do is claim salvation through acceptance of Jesus Christ, the Son of God, as my Savior. The next thing I would do is pray and wait upon the Lord for, "the prayer of faith shall save the sick, and the Lord shall raise him up; and if he have committed sins, they shall be forgiven him" (James 5:15).

Concurrently, I would deliberately withdraw myself from anything which would bind me to my old habits: lovers, friends, books, magazines, sensual clothing. Anything. Everything. And, I would seek help from a Bible preaching, Bible believing pastor or Christian counselor, a Christian psychiatrist or psychologist. But I would be watchful, lest I put more trust in them than Christ.

Yet Christian fellowship is vital.

If my Christian guide, however, began to teach me that my sin was acceptable, that I need not repent and recant my homosexuality, I would break off my counsel immediately and seek help elsewhere. I would be able to make this judgment because I would read my Bible daily with the help of competent study aids such as *Unger's Bible Commentary, Matthew Henry's Commentary* or any of the other works which have shown their reliability over a period of time. Second Timothy 3:16 states, "All scripture is given by inspiration of God, and is profitable for doctrine, for reproof, for correction, for instruction in righteousness."

Lastly, I would not expect too much too soon. It takes years of complicated environmental influences and personal choices, both conscious and subconscious, to make a person gay. The healing, also, might be a long process. I would take it a step at a time. I would not expect to be made "heterosexual" overnight. A heterosexual love might never be granted me. I would expect only to commune with my Lord and Master and seek His will in my life.

No, I would not worry about what future homosexual temptation might lay ahead, I would concentrate only on refraining from homosexual practices this day. Today's struggle with the devil will be taxing enough.

But we can fight the devil and win for the Bible confirms, "Resist the devil, and he will flee from you" (James 4:7).

I am not suggesting that any homosexual is that way because the devil made him do it. Satan will merely try to utilize the weakness of man's own flesh to keep man from God. He will use our lusts, our mistakes and our guilt to suppress our ability to reach out and embrace Christ's love.

Satan seeks to substitute his own bogus brand of gay liberation. But the good of gay liberation is not in the vanity of

"Gay is Proud." The good of gay liberation is not in demonstrations or coalitions or defense funds or humanism. The good of gay liberation is not in a positive self-image for homosexuals. These things only serve to further enslave those who would be free.

But in the righteous hands of Christ, "liberation" is a good thing, for He sets one truly at liberty. He liberates the gay from sin.

In Christ, the homosexual can be redeemed; can be cured.

But the Gay Invaders strike out at this truth every chance they get. They scoff at God and His holy Word. Where are they leading us as a nation? Where are they leading you?

Yes, the Gay Invaders march on.

March on.

March on.

How do we launch a counterattack?

13
The Turning of Things Right Side Up

On a sunny Saturday morning as I worked on this book, the phone in my den rang.

It was a friend of mine, a film maker, who wanted me to "stop whatever you are doing," and view the final print of his latest epic just back from the processing laboratory.

I declined his kind invitation, mumbling that I was working on the final pages of a manuscript due at the publishers' the following Monday.

"What are you writing about?" he asked innocently.

I told him the title.

"Good gravy!" he exclaimed. "What are you saying about that?"

As briefly as I could, I outlined some of the thoughts which I have included in these pages. It was with a little dread on my part, since homosexuality is not the usual subject for a Saturday morning chat.

But my friend was most interested. As a young man, he had been a professional musician. As had I, he had encountered homosexuals firsthand and close-up at a time when most people considered them as remote as men on Mars.

"You know," he said, "sometimes I worry about my two daughters." The girls are aspiring actresses in their late teens and early twenties. "Some of the friends they bring home scare me to death. I'm just not sure about them."

I sympathized.

"What do you think of Anita Bryant?" he asked.

"I like what she did," I said.

"So do I," he said. And that surprised me, because my friend is ecumenical in nature. He has been professionally involved in the arts for years. He is truly a Renaissance man. He writes, he composes, he produces and directs. He has had at least one film aired over a major television network. His home is constantly filled with bright, witty guests, some quite critical of organized religion. He is one of the most authentic intellectuals I have ever met.

And, let's face it, evangelical Christian stands are seldom popular with the intellectual class. But this man could not say enough about the evangelical woman who stood up for God and decency. He went on about her courage and the "excellent substance" of her position for several minutes.

When we hung up, I sat for a long while thanking God that there are people of all classes and intellects who *do* care, who are concerned about the inroads being made by the Gay Invaders.

And I thought about his daughters and about my own, a precocious seven-year-old with a bright, shining face and big brown eyes. A little girl who places so much trust in her daddy and his generation to protect her and her brother and all her friends from the evils of life.

And I thought of these things with my friend's last unanswered question still echoing through my brain:

"How do we stop it?"

For one thing, we have numbers on our side.

According to population estimates, there are between 50.1 million and 55 million evangelical Christians in the United States today. From this we probably should subtract ten percent, the figure which is supposed to be the percentage of homosexuals in *any* and *all* organizations. I am not sure the percentage is nearly that high in conservative Christian circles, but for statistical argument, let us give the benefit of the doubt.

By the most conservative estimate, then, we are left with 45.8 million people that profess belief in God's Word as the law of life; 45.8 million Bible-believing fundamental Christians.

If there are, as claimed, twenty million homosexuals in the United States, we evangelicals out-number them more than two to one! And that is a veritable army of Might to battle the Gay Invaders. And, if we could just recruit ten percent of the remaining U.S. population, people like my film maker friend, we would have an army of Right numbering more than fifty-nine million people—an edge of almost three to one!

But numbers and armies are only valuable if they are mobilized. And, I am afraid that is where we fall far short.

In the last presidential election, the difference between the winning candidate and the losing candidate was a margin of only two percent of the popular vote. In other words, about 1.75 million ballots.

Politicians live or die by such small margins these days that a few votes do make a difference. That is why they spend so much time courting special interest groups within the American fabric. That is why representatives of the twenty million avowed homosexuals were invited to the White House in 1977.

The gays are a well-organized and politically militant group. Our political leaders have good reason to believe that they can deliver their block of votes en masse.

Evangelicals, conversely, are generally disorganized when it comes to applying political pressure. We are too caught up in our parochial differences concerning minor doctrines and petty traditions. We should concentrate instead on the common cause of our Lord in the world.

When we are united, the results can be amazing.

By way of example, look at what happened when Anita Bryant took her stand in Dade County, Florida, and, under pressure from homosexuals at the national level, she was fired as host of a proposed television series for a major sewing machine manufacturer.

Evangelicals and their allies fought back with "tens of thousands" of letters and telephone calls protesting her dismissal. The company claimed that Miss Bryant's removal from its television show was done without top-level management approval and reinstated her. They insisted that public pressure had nothing to do with it. Perhaps it did not, but all those calls and letters certainly did no harm.

In mid-April, 1977, a circuit court judge declared the controversial ordinance "constitutional," thus appearing to clear the way for either repeal by the county commission or the voter referendum on the ordinance as sought by Save Our Children, the group backing Miss Bryant. The vote on the ordinance was set for June 7. When the smoke cleared and the tally was in, the ordinance had been repealed by a vote of approximately two to one. Yet the fight was not finished. Both sides vowed to continue it on a national level with homosexuals predicting passage of a federal law similar to the defeated Dade County ordinance. Evangelicals can be proud of their part in the nationwide support accorded to the anti-homosexual drive.

Yet such successful protests are rarely as spontaneous as was that surrounding the Dade County affair. It takes time to build an effective organization and if the trends are continued, time is short.

The place for Christians to begin this organization is probably with their own church. We should make certain that the truth about homosexuality is being taught there. If not, if the doctrine is being taught that homosexuality is normal or but a variation of normal, a protest should be lodged immediately with the pastor and other church leaders.

Then, a class or seminar on homosexuality should be staged by the church. It should be taught by a pastor or lay leader who has made a study of the facts and can present them without sensationalism or emotion. The teachings of the Bible on the subject should remain the center and the foundation of any such course. Representatives of other churches and community service organizations could be invited to attend.

Ideally, a steering committee should be formed with members from all the like-minded churches in a given locale. This committee would study the gay situation in its community, issue reports, and undertake a gospel ministry to homosexuals in its area of influence.

Almost every large city has a gay ghetto where homosexual bars and businesses are more dense than any other place in the metropolitan area. A special missionary endeavor might be launched into that ghetto to acquaint homosexuals with the Word of God and the grace of Christ. It would be preferable that these missionaries themselves be former homosexuals who have repented and are firmly in Christ. In any event, those who undertake such a ministry should do so with care and

Christian sharing. It should be a mission of Christlike love much more than pious condemnation.

The steering committee might also arrange periodic meetings with senators and congressional representatives at both the federal and state levels to lobby for the Christian point-of-view. Similar meetings should also be planned and staged with city councilmen, mayors, police and county supervisors.

Another project for the steering committee might be the establishment and funding of a "Gay Crisis Line," manned by trained volunteers who could counsel and pray with troubled homosexuals.

Whenever an important bill or ordinance is to come before one of the lawmaking bodies, the steering committee should arrange for mass demonstrations and rallies complete with banners and placards. In such instances, the press should also be invited.

Quite a vision. It's right out of the Gay Libbers' book, except, in reverse. But why not for Christians? Why can't it work? Because Christians are too busy spreading the Word, feeding and caring for the hungry, the sick and the lame. We have too many other projects and concerns to spend all our time fighting the Gay Invasion. But that doesn't mean we can't do something and be successful on the homosexual front. After all, our power and support come from God.

I do think a class within the local church on homosexuality is necessary. It is vital that people understand the scope and individual character of the thing called homosexuality. We must get back to the Bible as a society, and the church is the best place for that reform to begin.

Beyond that, as an individual Christian, letter writing is a potent lobbying tool. It is something we all can and should do. Find out the name of your congressman and senator and write whenever an issue concerning homosexuality comes before Congress. I know all this sounds trite, but it works.

And when you write to any politician don't feel you have to compose a long essay on your view. The sad truth is, the average politician is not going to read all of it anyway. What he or she does care about, is how many pieces did he get *for* an issue, how many *against*.

Your letter can be as short and sweet as this:

Dear_____:

I am against the proposed measure for homosexual rights. I take this stand out of my deep religious and moral convictions.

Sincerely,

You see? You don't even have to tell him you're not going to vote for him in the next election if he does not follow your advice. And there is no rule which says you cannot write more than one letter. The more times you write on an individual issue, the better. All the politician will probably know is that seven hundred letters were received in favor of such-and-such a measure, only three hundred and two pieces of mail were opposed.

It's numbers, not substance which count. And as with Congress, so with the White House. Write, write, write. And, if you have the time and money and really want to make your opinion known, telephone. The operator on the switchboard, whether it is the White House, the Congress, the State Legislator or your local mayor's office, will most likely have been instructed to keep à "log" of all calls, pro and con.

Know the facts. Facts come from reading and being informed. Most news about gays is not on page one or two. Sometimes the most significant kind of story, such as one about a White House meeting with homosexual representatives, will be buried at the back of the paper.

And when you discover something which demands Christian action, do not assume that everyone else has discovered it, too. Share your knowledge with your pastor and other church officials, your Sunday School class, your friends and neighbors. Urge them to join you in protesting through the mails and over the phone.

Circulate petitions. Get signatures. Numbers.

Don't overlook the letters-to-the-editor column of newspapers. Community leaders and folks in general do read these columns regularly. They can be a great aid in helping to turn the tide of public opinion in our favor.

But the best way to influence a newspaper is to cancel your

subscription in writing with carbon copies of your letter sent to the paper's advertising manager and to its major advertisers. The letter should be constructed something like this:

Dear Circulation Manager:

> Due to your newspaper's continued support of certain abnormal lifestyles including the practice of homosexuality, please cancel my subscription at once.
>
> I am sending copies of this letter to your advertisers to inform them that as long as they continue to advertise with you, I will not do business with them.
>
> This action is not taken with malice, but out of a deep Christian concern for the future moral well-being of our society.
>
> Thank you,

One such letter won't make much of a difference. But tens of letters for the same cause will make them think. Hundreds of letters will make them act.

As for the advertisers who might receive a copy of your letters—well, I have had clients who literally questioned entire campaigns over a single postcard of criticism. To the officials of a firm like that, ten letters can seem like an avalanche and a hundred letters a cataclysm. As difficult as it is these days for any kind of business to survive the pressures of competition, the thing most businesses do not want is a consumer revolt due to a controversy not of their making. They prefer to maintain a low profile because it is "safe."

The same technique will work on magazines, radio and television.

However, I do not think news coverage relating to gays should be protested, unless it is so needlessly sensational as to be offensive. I believe protest should be aimed at those who editorialize for homosexuality as "normal." We need legitimate news. but not illegitimate opinion in the guise of news.

Remember, too, it is not the gay *individual* we strive against, but the homosexual *practice*. And the spreading myth surrounding that practice.

The men and women who are the real victims of the Gay Invasion are the homosexuals themselves. If after hearing the gospel, they turn a deaf ear and continue their practices in private, there is nothing more that we as Christians can do.

Under the law of our land, they have a right to be left to their own devices. But as that right applies to them, it also should apply to us.

They must be made to realize that we have the right to protect our values, our homes, our families, our children against their philosophy of Sodom. We want things left right side up for ourselves and those that are ours.

No, we cannot, must not hate the homosexual. But we must stand against their propaganda and their flaunting of things dark.

As we have seen, homosexuality is a sin, nurtured primarily by environment and habit. If a homosexual repents and confesses to Christ, we must not look at him or her and whisper to our brethren, "There goes a homosexual." For if they are made whole in Christ, they are no longer guilty sinners but saved sinners just as you and I. We must learn to view them through the blood of Christ and that means with total forgiveness. Follow the example of the Jesus who died for us who said unto the sinner, "Neither do I condemn thee: go, and sin no more" (John 8:11).

Follow the example of the men of faith who followed Him, our forefathers in Christ who believed, "And be ye kind one to another, tenderhearted, forgiving one another, even as God for Christ's sake hath forgiven you" (Ephesians 4:32).

The best weapons against the Gay Invasion are Christian charity and Christian knowledge.

Arm yourself.

An Afterword

No campaign against the spreading abnormality in our society will be successful unless it begins in the heart and in the home.

Jesus preached, "Blessed are the pure in heart: for they shall see God" (Matthew 5:8).

I once heard a great preacher and Bible expositor say, "I don't preach many sermons on hell, because I think if you tell men that is where they are going, you must feel a genuine sorrow for them in your heart. You must not wish them evil, but wish them well."

King David prayed, "Create in me a clean heart, O God: and renew a right spirit within me" (Psalms 51:10).

So before we can heal the world, we must heal our own hearts and cleanse them from our sins through prayer and confession to our Lord.

And then, we must establish in our children a reverence for God's holy law. As I have labored on this work, I have reached the conclusion that our children are so apt to be exposed to the Gay Invasion very early in their lives that we must in some manner prepare them to deal with it.

My own children are ten and seven. When I first began to research and write on the subject of homosexuality, I sought to keep them entirely ignorant of what I was doing. But it came to me that once the book was published one of their friends at school or even church, whose parents are not as cautious as their mother and I, might well confront them with it. Somehow, someway, I had to prepare them.

My wife and I discussed it and prayed about it and these are the words which I believe God gave me:

"You know Daddy is writing a new book," I said.

"Yeah," my son said. "What is the story about?"

"It is not a story book," I said. "It's a book about something God doesn't like very well. It will be titled, 'The Gay Invasion.'"

" 'The Gay De-vashun,' " my daughter mouthed. "What's that mean?"

I took a deep breath. This was the moment of truth. "Well, kids," I said. "The word 'gay' is sometimes used to talk about a homosexual. A homosexual is a man who loves a man or a woman who loves a woman as Daddy and Mommy love each other."

They thought it over a moment.

"You mean a man and a man kiss?" my son asked.

"Something like that," I answered.

"Uck!"

"Now you might hear some people say on television or someday in school that being gay or homosexual is okay. But it is not. God says it is wrong. Very wrong. A bad thing to do. And that's what Daddy is writing his book about. I'm trying to tell people how wrong God says it is."

"Good idea," my son said.

"Good idea, Daddy," my daughter parroted. And off they went to play, after I had warned them not to discuss the subject with any of their friends, unless those friends mentioned it first.

But had I succeeded in making them understand what so many adults cannot grasp? The most difficult thing for a parent to do in situations like this is to *trust* in the Lord. I tried. Still, in the back of my mind, I could not help but have some honest doubts.

A few nights later, we were watching the early news on television when, without warning, they presented a story with homosexual references.

My children were playing a game on the floor. I hoped they were too busy to notice.

But my little girl looked up. "They're talking about 'homosexual,' Dad. And I know what that is. It's wrong."

Praise the Lord.

Yet I know my fight for their souls and the souls of Christian children everywhere is not won. There will be other battles, other confrontations with forces not of our making.

Writing this now, I think of First John 4:4: "Ye are of God, little children, and have overcome them: because greater is he that is in you, than he that is in the world.''

Greater is He.

We will overcome.

We will.

Amen.